Just Us Girls II

A Bible Study on Finding Your Confidence In Middle School

D1279936

Just Us Girls II

A Bible Study on Finding Your Confidence In Middle School

HANNAH DUGGAN

CROSS
HILL
PRESS

ISBN 10: 197399674X
ISBN 13: 9781973996743

PRAISE FOR *JUST US GIRLS*

"Hannah's heart for girls seeps through the pages! *Just Us Girls* points each girl, regardless of her age or circumstances to Jesus, the Anchor of her soul."

-Kelsey Erich

Youth Leader, Calvary Chapel Honolulu

"As a senior pastor's wife, I was able to see fresh ways to approach young ladies as I gained insights from Hannah. *Just Us Girls* offers big sisterly advice and practical road signs of what to expect ahead."

-Kathy Newman

Women's Ministry Leader, Calvary Chapel Windward

"The girls are WOWED that it hits every single struggle they face as middle schoolers. I knew this would be a good one; I wasn't aware it would be the best one to pick!"

-Amazon Reviewer

"This book is perfect for any junior high girl. Fast paced witty humor that will hold attention and help point them to the purpose God has for them. This book is going to be a great tool used at Calvary Chapel Bend."

-Matt and Shari Ferguson

Youth Leaders at Calvary Chapel Bend

"As a mom, I found *Just Us Girls* relatable and engaging. Girls will be blessed by Hannah's been-there-done-that-and-lived-through-it narrative."

-Keren Stonebraker

Ministry Leader, South Shore Christian Fellowship

"As a young woman Hannah has a way of connecting with girls where they are at and challenging them to a deeper maturity with each other and in their relationship with Jesus. I highly recommend *Just Us Girls!*"

-Amazon Reviewer

PRAISE FOR HANNAH DUGGAN

"Hannah is a legend! Read. Her. Book. Actually, you don't read her book. It reads you as it dares one to be the warrior God has empowered one to be."

-Pastor Ben Courson

Applegate Christian Fellowship

"I've read *From the Flames* and found it to be a fascinating read! I was not only extremely impressed, but equally blessed by Hannah's words. The Lord's hand is upon this young lady!"

-Pastor Mike Stangel

North Shore Christian Fellowship

"*Dare Greatly* covers everything from stress to sharing your faith, and it's really inspired me to draw closer to God, to achieve His standards instead of everybody else's."

-Elizabeth Newsom

Blogger

"Hannah's work is theologically rich and imaginatively illustrative, making it one of the easiest challenging books I have read in a long time. People of the millennial generation will find their souls being spoken to by someone who is undoubtedly a prophet for our time."

-Author Wavey Cowpar

"Hannah Duggan writes with passion and clarity about life's big questions in an engaging, thoughtful, and fun manner. Full of personal stories, penetrating questions, and practical examples, this book is an awesome guide for young people."

-Author Jebraun Clifford

OTHER BOOKS BY HANNAH DUGGAN

DEVOTIONALS AND BIBLE STUDIES

What Now?

*The Young Adult's Practical, Spiritual, and
Somewhat Unusual Guide to Finding God's Will*

Dare Greatly:

A High School Girl's Bible Study on Thriving in Your Teens

Just Us Girls:

A Bible Study on Being God's Girl in Middle School

Just Us Girls II:

A Bible Study on Finding Your Confidence in Middle School

FICTION

Dear Kate: A Novel

From the Flames: A Novel

For the dream chasers,
world changers, and warriors,
who dared to be God's girls in middle school.

CONTENTS

INTRODUCTION

When I wrote a twelve-week Bible study called *Just Us Girls*, I never imagined how many girls it would reach. I didn't know then, how many girls would share the stories, their griefs, and their struggles with me. I had no idea how many girls would rise to the challenge of being God's girl in middle school. Over the last three years, I have met so many incredible young women. They are beautiful, passionate warriors for the kingdom. They are starting Bible studies and sharing Jesus with their friends and discovering who they are. As I emailed and chatted with girls all over the world, I noticed that they had something in common.

While these girls were pursuing God, and striving to be the young women God created them to be, they were losing their confidence. The pressures of school, friends, and boys had started to get to them.

"I wish I looked like her."

"The boys in my class say I'm annoying."

"My best friend won't talk to me."

Each time I heard their stories, I flashed back to my own middle school experience. I remembered feeling awkward, nervous, and insecure, terrified that no one would like me.

Already, the world was trying to steal the beautiful person each of these girls was becoming. It was trying to steal their confidence.

How many of us carry around the insults, embarrassments, and insecurities we collected in middle school?

How many of us sill cringe at the things we said when we were twelve?

How many of us lost our confidence at age eleven?

How many of us still haven't found it?

Our God has promised His daughters security and confidence. We were not created to live in insecurity. We were created to live a limitless adventure of faith.

That adventure doesn't need to start in two years or five years or ten. We can be strong, confident, bold young women right now.

These twelve chapters discuss twelve areas of insecurity that every middle school girl deals with. This book covers everything from self-worth to finding your secret weapon. How do you deal with bullies? What do you when your crush doesn't like you back? How should you choose your friends? The answers to all of these questions are found in God's Word, and together, we're going to find out what the Scriptures have to say about our confidence.

Each chapter is equipped with five daily devotions designed to draw us closer to God day by day.

All you will need for this study is a Bible, a journal, and some pens.

If you are an individual reading this book...

...then, girl, it's you and me! Consider this our weekly

Bible study. We'll dig into God's Word and talk about the things that try to steal our confidence. I encourage you to participate in the daily devotions in order to get the most out of this book. If we're going to let the Scriptures change us from the inside out, we need to fully engage. If we're going to win our confidence back, we can't just show up once a week. We need to walk with our Savior daily. Read the Scriptures and answer the questions found in the Daily Study Guides to truly soak in everything that God would say to us in the next twelve weeks.

If you are a Bible study leader...

...I am so excited to share this book with you. I've found that the best way to use this book in a group setting is to read the chapters together, and assign the Study Guides as weekly homework.

I know how hard it can be to find materials for your girls. You'll find loads of resources, including printable memory verses, the *Just Us Girls II: Leader Guide*, and fun ideas for games and ice-breakers on my website:

www.authorhannahduggan.wordpress.com

If you are a first-time Bible study leader, you can also download my free PDF Book, *How to Lead a Teen Bible Study (And Not Die): Five Things Every Youth Leader Should Know.*

If you would like to connect with other groups participating in this study, you can post pictures of your group and your projects on social media using the hashtag:

#justusgirlsstudy

To get free Bible study materials, enter fun contests, and get exclusive looks at my latest books, you can sign up for my newsletter.

Connecting with Bible study groups is one of the best parts of my job. I would love to email your girls, skype with your group, or even come to do a retreat at your church. If you would be interested in arranging a time where I can connect with your Bible study group, you can email me at:

authorhannahduggan@gmail.com

As a Bible study leader myself, I know the struggles that you face. I am so honored to be serving alongside you to raise up the warriors of this next generation. Never forget how eternal your work is. I am in youth ministry today because of the Godly leaders who poured into my life when I was in middle school. You have no idea what God will do behind the scenes as you are doing His work. Thank you so much for taking this journey with me.

Middle school is a rough road, but if we cling to our Savior, our middle school experience can be the first step in a glorious walk of expectant faith. I am so excited for each of us to find our confidence as we search God's Word and discover who He created us to be. If we choose to take in all God has for, this experience will root us so deeply into God's love that we will never be the same. Are you ready to find your confidence?

Let's get started!

CHAPTER 1

With Great Power
Comes Great Identity

Grace and peace be multiplied to you
In the knowledge of God and of Jesus our Lord,
As His divine power has given to us all things
That pertain to life and godliness,
Through the knowledge of Him who called us
By glory and virtue.

2 PETER 1:2-3

A Chapter on Finding Your Secret Weapon

WARNING

This book may contain concentrated amounts of self-confidence, dangerously powerful secret weapons, and classified information that could lead to the ultimate destruction of insecurity. This book is only to be handled by middle school girls with the utmost responsibility. *Just Us Girls* is not liable for the explosive nature of the personal transformations that may occur. Read on...if you dare.

Wow! You dared. I'm impressed.

If you're here with me on this page, you are most likely in middle school, and your life is crazy hard. How do I know this? I can read minds. (Ha! Gotchya. Not really.) I know that your life is hard, because middle school is crazy hard for everyone. I remember it well.

One day you're a content little kid who's got your life together.

Then BAM! Puberty hits ya like a bus and you lay there in

a pile of emotions and pimples wondering what just happened.

Your life feels like it's spiraling down the drains of drama.

Boys (who used to fall very clearly into the "gross" category) are now an entirely new species of human. Still gross...but also kind of cute. (When did that happen?!)

You're covered in bruises (and probably whatever you last spilled down the front of your shirt) because you've grown about three inches since yesterday, and you feel like you're walking around in someone else's body. Where did these long legs come from?! Whose hair is this? Is that MY voice?!

The result of all this? We want nothing more than to hide under the bed until our sweet sixteen. Middle school is the time when we come face-to-face with the ugly monster of insecurity, when our self-confidence takes a hit. Thoughts start to creep in. Thoughts like...

"Maybe I'm not funny. Maybe I'm just annoying."

"Look at me. What boy is going to notice me?"

"I wish I looked like her."

"What if no one likes me, and everyone just puts up with me?"

If we're not careful, these thoughts have the power to wreck our self-confidence for years to come. There are women who are still plagued by the self-doubt that haunted them in middle school.

You and I were not meant to live like that.

You and I were meant to be shining lights in a dark world. Jesus didn't just tell that to adults. He meant it for you, right now, in middle school. You don't have to wait to grow into your self-confidence. You can be the bold, sparkling personality that God created you to be. In the next twelve weeks, you and I are going to find our confidence. We're going to discover the tools and weapons we've been given as children of God. We are going to dig so deep into His Word that we will never be the same. If we truly focus on what God has for us in these twelve chapters, our insecurities will have no place left to hide. We will be transformed into the confident young women we were meant to be.

Consider yourself warned.

Discovering Your Power

If you've read the first *Just Us Girls*, you know how much I love a good movie, particularly something adventurous. I'm a huge fan of super hero movies, and not just any super hero movies. My favorites are the origin stories. You know the ones. Your average human wakes up one day and realizes that they are different, special, and blessed with super-human abilities. They then embark on a quest to discover why they were chosen and what they are capable of. This usually involves a mysterious letter, an ultra-wise mentor, or a school for gifted youngsters.

As a child of the Living God, you have already been accepted into the Beloved (Ephesians 1:6). You were chosen before the foundations of the earth (Ephesians 1:4). The power that raised Jesus from the dead flows through your spiritual veins (Ephesians 1:19-20). In other words, you, sweet girl, have been blessed with superhuman abilities. It's time to realize who you are and what you're capable of.

Wait! Before you go jump out of a tree you should finish this chapter. You *do* have super human abilities, however, as a matter of full disclosure you should know that this does not give you the ability to fly, climb walls, or fight crime single-handedly.

Okay. Now that we've gotten that out of the way it's time to figure out what your super powers really are. When you've received Jesus into your heart, you become an adopted child of God, and that means that you've inherited some awesome abilities from your Heavenly Father. Here are just a few:

1. You're immortal. Yup. Jesus came that we may have life more abundantly (John 10:10). If Jesus dwells within you, sister, you and I are going to live forever with Him (Revelation 22:5) at the party called Heaven where each one of us is invited.

2. You're spiritually invincible. WAIT! Put the nun-chucks down. You heard me. Put 'em down. There will be no vigil-anti Bible study groups tonight. I do not want to get letters mothers who sent their daughters to Bible study and ended up with a crime-fighting gang. Yes, you are invincible, *spiritually*. This means that nothing the Devil throws at you is ever going to work (Isaiah 54:17). It might knock you down, but you've got God on your side, and you are going to pull yourself up and get back in that game no matter what Satan or this world tries to do (Proverbs 24:16).

3. You are free. We hear people say this a lot, but if we've been raised in the church we might not fully grasp what it means. Free? Free from what? Free from every darkness. Free from sin. Free from guilt and shame. Free from the

lies of this world. When Jesus became Lord of your life, He set you free (John 8:36). When we repent of all that we have done wrong, our sin is thrown as far as the East is from the West (Psalm 103:12). When we start to despair over this world or this life, Jesus has promised to be our joy (John 15:11).

All superheroes, mutants, and otherwise gifted individuals have one thing in common: a purpose. They're journey is one of discovery. Over the course of their adventure they learn why they have been given these gifts, and how to use them for a very specific calling. You and I are no different. We have been given a commission by our Commander in Chief. We have a specific purpose given to us in Isaiah Chapter 61. We are called to...

- Preach good news to the poor.
- Heal broken hearts.
- Tell other captives that they are free.
- Bring liberty to those who are oppressed.

You and I have a mission. It's our choice whether or not we're going to accept it.

Self Defense

No super hero story would be complete without a training montage. That music kicks in, and the heroes-in-training learn to use the power they've been given.

In this life, you are going to come up against a lot of

resistance. Our Enemy, the Devil, prowls this earth like a roaring lion (1 Peter 5:8). There are lots of Christians that live in the fear of this Enemy, but you and I have no need to be afraid. Our God has defeated that Enemy already, and he can roar all he likes, but he has no power over God's kids.

However, this doesn't stop him from trying to trip us up. Your Enemy can't control you or own you, but *girl*, he can distract you. Our Enemy controls the darkness of this world, and you and I need to be ready for his attacks. We cannot be ignorant of the weapons he will use against us (2 Corinthians 2:11).

He will tell you that you are not good enough.

He will tell you that God does not love you.

He will tell you that you're better off hiding under your bed for the next five years.

He is the Father of Lies, and he lies to us on a daily basis. Our best defense against this is the battle suit given to us in Ephesians Chapter 6. Armed to the teeth with the truth, righteousness, peace, faith, and the salvation of Jesus, we are told that our best weapon is the Word of God. Those Bible verses your Sunday school teacher made you memorize aren't just one more assignment. They are the weapons that will win you the victory.

Your Secret Identity

Whether you're a reporter for the Daily Planet, a mild-mannered scientist, or a middle school girl, every hero needs a secret identity. By day, you might sit in that classroom, innocent as Peter Parker himself, but what your classmates don't know is that there is another side to you. You have a secret identity in Christ. Your friends, the bullies, and even your teachers don't know who you really are. They might know that you're a Christian, but they don't know that the power of God resides inside you. They don't know that you battle it out with the powers of darkness on a regular basis. They don't know that middle school is just another way for you to carry out your mission to set people free. To them, you're just a mild-mannered middle school girl, but you and I know better.

If you grew up watching *The Incredibles*, you'll remember the scene when Mrs. Incredible tells her kids to use the powers they've been given. She then warns them about the danger of their Enemy. She informs them that he will not go easy on them just because they're children. She then gives each of her kids a mask and tells them that their identity is their most precious possession.

Your identity as a daughter of the Living God is your most precious possession. This world will try to steal it from you, saying that you are just like everybody else. You need to remember who you are to your Heavenly Father. To Jesus, you were worth dying for. If we can hold that in our minds, no bully will ever be able to get us down, no insult will ever stick in our minds, and nothing will ever steal the identity we have in Christ.

Gadgets and Tech

Another iconic scene from any adventure story is the moment when the mentor leads the hero down the mysterious, spiral staircase to a secret room. *Click.* The light goes on, and there, wall-to-wall is the cutting-edge technology that is all available to the hero.

In these pages, you and I are going to take a trip down

the spiral staircase of Scripture. (Why a spiral staircase? Because why have a normal staircase when you could have a mysterious, spiral one?) In these pages, we are going to discover the wall-to-wall promises of God.

Click.

Joy that nothing can ever dampen (Philippians 4:4).

Peace that no one can ever steal (Philippians 4:7)

Wisdom whenever you want it (James 1:5).

Courage that withstands any storm (Romans 8:28).

Confidence in the love of Jesus Christ (Ephesians 3:12)

Those are just a few of the cutting-edge tools available to you!

2 Peter 1:3 tells us that we have been given all that we need for life and godliness. The best part about these gadgets? They're not just for the grown-ups. These are your tools. You and I are going to spend the next twelve weeks learning how to use them. When life has got you down, when you want to hide from the rest of the world, you remember who you are. You might not fit in, but guess what?! You were not made to fit in. You were chosen to be the powerful daughter of an Invincible God.

Your training begins now.

With Great Power
Come Great Identity
Daily Study Guide

Day 1

Read 2 Peter 1:3

   A. How many things has God given us for life and godliness? According to the verse, how do we get these things?

   B. King Solomon was once told to ask God for anything. If God told you to ask for anything, what you ask for?

   C. This verse in 2 Peter doesn't say that God has given us whatever we want. He's given us whatever we *need* in order to live lives that please God. What do you feel like your Christian walk is missing? Do you need patience, bravery, confidence? God wants you to ask Him for these things. Spend time in prayer, asking God for whatever it is that you need in your spiritual life, and be prepared to share it with your group.

DAY 2
Read Isaiah 61:1

A. What four things has God anointed us to do? According to this verse, how can we do these things?

B. What do these four things look like in real life? Have you ever seen one of your Godly mentors heal broken hearts? Have you ever heard of Christian heroes who set captives free? Be prepared to share these stories with your group.

C. Just like we talked about in the chapter, all of us have been given a mission by God. These four missions make up our mission. We're called to tell the captives of this lost world that they can be free if they follow Jesus. What part of this mission sounds the hardest to you? What might keep you from fulfilling your mission?

DAY 3
Read Ephesians 6:11-12

A. What will protect us against the wiles of the Devil? What four things do we wrestle against?

B. What do you think is the most important part of self-defense? How do you think Scripture can be used as a weapon?

C. Get out your paper and your pencils. I want you to draw your best battle suit. It can be ancient suit of armor, like Ephesians 6 describes. Or it can be a futuristic super suit. Be ready to explain how it protects you from the Devil and keeps you focused on God. Get creative! (Your youth leader can post pictures of your battle suits using the hashtag #justusgirlsstudy so I can see your creations!)

DAY 4
Read Ephesians 1:4

A. When did God choose you? According to this verse, why?

B. Have you ever been chosen for something special? What was it? How did it make you feel?

C. Today, as you go about your routine remember your secret identity. You're not just an average middle school girl. You are an agent of Heaven. This means that throughout the day, you need to keep your eyes open for missions the Lord might send your way. Is there someone you can encourage? Is there a way you could secretly bless someone? Be ready to share how your missions went this week with your Bible study group.

DAY 5
Read 2 Corinthians 1:20

A. What two words are used to describe the promises of God in this verse? What does the glory of God flow through, according to this verse?

B. The Bible is full of the promises of God. What are two things that God has promised us in His Word?

C. Your challenge today is to start believing God's promises. Do you have trouble trusting Him to provide for you? Do you doubt His love for you? Do you fear that He won't come through in the future? If we are experiencing fear or doubt, it's because we're not truly believing in God's promises. Discover which promises you have trouble believing, and pray that God will show you how to take Him at His Word.

CHAPTER 2

Breaking Free of the Box

For whoever desires to save his life will lose it,
But whoever loses his life for My sake
Will find it.

MATTHEW 16:25

A Chapter on Embracing the Real You

Pink Ribbon Rage

Maddy was one cool twelve-year-old. I could tell from her jacket, her ripped jeans, and the way she stood on the fringes of the room, rolling her eyes at me.

"Are you here for our class?" I asked as her two younger sisters skipped into the fray of ballet dancers I was about to teach.

She shot a disgusted look at me over her phone. "Seriously?"

I forced a smile. "Okay. Why don't you take a seat over there where you can watch your sisters?"

With one more roll of her eyes, she schlumped across the room and sat her too-cool booty down.

Oh, yeah. This was going to be fun.

There was a lot I didn't know about Maddy. I couldn't have guessed that she was currently living in a tent. I couldn't have guessed that she was the only thing holding her broken family together. And I certainly couldn't have

17

guessed what she would do next.

As I taught a dance class of frolicking little girls, I could sense her eye-rolling, dance-mocking presence behind me. At the beginning of the class she laughed at her sisters, mocked their attempts to dance, and shot me a few death-glares.

Nice.

As class wore on, she quieted, watching the little twirling pink tornadoes with the same, sour expression but less vocally.

In the dance class I taught, there was a moment which every girl lived in hope of. It was the pinnacle, the height of the junior ballerina existence. As I reached into my basket of magical tricks, I produced thirteen pink ribbons, and the room dissolved into excitement. Little girls giggled, clapped, and bobbed in place. The time had come to run across the floor to the tunes of *Frozen*, and take a flying leap over a Hello-Kitty stuffed animal. What did the pink ribbons do? Absolutely nothing. But when you're eight, life doesn't get better than twirling a pink ribbon, jumping over a stuffed cat, and singing loud enough for all of Arandelle to hear. As we handed out twelve pink ribbons to twelve expectant little be-tutued girls, I struggled to keep them in a straight line and make them wait their turn. I held the extra ribbon in my hand as I instructed them.

"No, you may not have two. Yes, I know they're magical, but it wouldn't be fair."

I shot a glance at Maddy, expecting another roll of her eyes. Instead, she sat on the other side of the room on the edge of her seat, mouth open, eyes fixed on the pink ribbon in my hand.

Well, that's weird. I turned back to my class (which

resembled a dozen dizzy butterflies trying to stand in a line). I explained the complicated technique of the feat they were about to undertake, and they listened with the utmost attention. (Actually, most of them were picking their noses, proving that they could sing louder than Queen Elsa, and shoving their sister, but I could imagine that they were listening.)

"You will jump over Hello-Kitty, all while twirling the pink silk ribbon above your—"

"I can't take it anymore!!" Maddy's voice ricocheted off the walls, and I turned around to see her making a bee-line for me. For two-tenths of a second, I feared for my life. Shoving her phone in her pocket she stretched out her hand. "I need a ribbon!" she shouted.

In a state of shock, I handed over the last ribbon, and watched as Maddy-the-Cool hopped in line behind her sisters and smiled for the first time that day. From that moment on, Maddy was one of the best dance student I ever had. Every week she came, ripped jeans, headphones in, and every week she smiled and twirled ribbons with the best of them.

There comes a moment in every girl's life, when she can't take it anymore, when the box she has built herself into doesn't fit.

The Unchangeables

Did you ever build a box fort when you were little? I remember mine vividly. My childhood fortress was made of impenetrable cardboard, colored with all kinds of marker, and big enough to hold a refrigerator. (No. Seriously, it was a refrigerator box.) I practically lived in my box fort until it was rained on, trampled, and left soggy in the back yard. (A moment of silence for my childhood dream house.)

Every girl lives in a box in her mind. Every girl's box looks different. Some boxes are constructed of ripped jeans and headphones, others of nail polish and lipstick. In our box, we cling to the things that make us unique. Our "style," the things we do, and the things we would *never* do. As life goes on the box shifts and changes.

Middle school is the time in our lives when we first create our box. It's our first chance to strut our stuff and show who we are. We scramble to find which box we fit into, and we stick there, sometimes for the rest of our lives. Heaven forbid we end up in the wrong box, or the weird box, or the box that people laugh at.

What does your box look like? Is it an unstoppable fortress? Is it covered in glitter? Is it made to look like everyone else's box? Do you even like the box you're in, or did you end up there without meaning to? Did you create your box, or did someone else create it for you?

Imagine that this was a project in school. If you had to display your personality in a box, how would you do it? What would it look like on the outside? What would it look like on the inside?

It's important that we don't confuse our confining box with the solid foundation of our life. There are things in each of our lives that anchor us. Things like our faith, our family, and our deepest desires. Everything else in our lives might change, but these are the unchangeables. They will always be a part of us.

The most important unchangeable is our relationship with Jesus.

My thirteenth birthday is one of my most precious

memories. In my quiet, home-loving family, birthdays are usually cozy family celebrations. However, the day I turned thirteen was another story. It was a coming-of-age celebration, not just for me, but for my friends as well. Our girls' Bible study discussed what we would wear, how we would do our hair, and who was coming to the party. In the midst of this preparation, my mom gave each of us an assignment. She gave us one verse:

He said to them,
"But who do you say that I am?"
Matthew 16:15

Before the party, each of us had to answer that question for ourselves. At the time, I didn't understand the connection, but looking back, it was one of the best things our girls' Bible study ever did. As we stretched our wings, our style, and found our place in life, each of us had to answer that question for ourselves.

Who do you say that Jesus is?

Your answer to this question will define the rest of your life.

Once we find our honest answer to this question, we need to determine what the unchangeables are in our life. In the next ten years, your life is going to change a lot. *You* are going to change a lot. If we can figure out what our unchangeables are, we will have something to hold onto even if life is spinning out of control.

Boxed In

It's not just our own insecurities that put us in a box. Society and culture try to box us in all the time, and too often, we let ourselves slip into these boxes.

Some of us fall into the bubbly and popular box.

Some of us choose to be the tough girl who can throw a football and take a hit.

Some of us just want to crawl into any box at all so we can fit in.

We are going to miss out on so much in life if we let ourselves be defined by cliques and popularity.

Don't let this world slap labels on that box of yours. You were not meant to simply be "the cool girl" or "the popular girl" or "the nerdy girl."

Just like Maddy, you and I need the courage to break out of the box, and try something new. If we don't, our lives will quickly become stale and confining.

Let the rest of the world scramble and search for their boxes. You were never created to fit a mold or live life from a box.

You were made to walk confidently.

You were created to be a young woman of passion and unashamed joy. That doesn't mean we walk around with a fake smile plastered over a bad attitude. It means that we sink our roots deep into who Jesus is.

Finding Your Sookay

Shortly after asking His disciples that life changing question, Jesus made one of the most powerful statements in the gospels.

For whoever desires to save his life will lose it,
But whoever loses his life for My sake

Will find it.
For what does it profit a man
If he gains the whole world, and loses his own soul?
Or what will a man give in exchange for his soul?
Matthew 16:25-26

This verse is referring to our eternal souls, but in that culture, your soul was not just the part of you that went to Heaven. Your soul is everything that gives you life. It's your spiritual breath, but it's also everything that makes you unique.

The word for "life" and the word for "soul" are the same word. The Greek word psyche (pronounced sookay). That word can mean "the part of you that lives forever," but it can also mean "the desires of your heart, the things you love, and the things you hate." In other words, your soul is the unique thumbprint of God that makes you different from everyone else in the world.

In middle school, everyone is trying to save their soul—their personality, their popularity, their likes, and their dislikes.

If you spend your middle school years trying to save your personality, honey, you're gonna lose it. I promise you. I have seen it happen so many times. In middle school, we strive to be the most fascinating person. We find our worth in one thing, whether that's music, makeup, sports, movies, or books. None of it lasts.

One day, you won't have time to put on that makeup.

One day, your life will not revolve around sports.

Those books, those movies, that music will not always be popular.

And when that happens, we will lose it.

So how do we find our soul?

It's hidden beneath the masks we wear, the insecurities we've created, and the boxes we hide in. Each one of us has a brilliant, one-of-a-kind God-given spark distinct from all creation. Do not exchange your sookay for what everyone else is chasing.

You were created to be the girl who shines.

You were made to be the girl who take the lead and stands apart from the crowd.

You were designed to know who you are and stand in it confidently.

It's time to break out of the box.

It's time to shove that phone in your pocket and allow yourself to take a flying leap out of your comfort zone.

It's time to let go of everything this world says you need and find yourself in Jesus Christ.

Jesus never asked you to be a cardboard cutout. He wants everyone.

He wants the skater girl who reads Shakespeare.

He wants the quiet girl who has a killer sense of humor.

He wants the popular girl who has a knack for algebra.

He wants the athlete who enjoys classical music.

He wants us to live lives free of confinement, out in the wide-open spaces of His grace. He wants you to break free of the box.

Breaking Free of the Box
Daily Study Guide

DAY 1
Read Matthew 16:13-14

A. What question did Jesus ask His disciples? What were some of the titles that people had assigned to Jesus?

B. Have you ever heard people say false things about Jesus? Who do people say Jesus is today?

C. Write out a list of what the Bible says about Jesus. (If you can include what verses back up your answers, extra points!)

DAY 2
Read Matthew 16:15-16

A. What question did Jesus ask His disciples? What was Peter's answer?

B. Who do you say that Jesus is, honestly, in your heart? How long have you believed this? What caused you to believe it?

C. That statement is one of our unchangeables that we discussed in the chapter. Get your pens and paper out and create a beautiful version of this statement. Hang it somewhere that you'll be able to see it, on your wall, or in the front of your binder to remind you of Who Jesus is.

DAY 3

Read Matthew 16:25

A. There is a great flip-flop statement in this verse. What is it? What is the original word for "life"? (Hint: We learned it in the previous chapter.)

B. Have you ever seen someone try so hard to save their soul (or personality) that they lost it completely? Has this ever happened to you?

C. This week, I challenge you to break out of the box. Try one thing that's outside of your box, something new that you wouldn't usually try!

DAY 4

Read Matthew 16:26

A. What trade is described in this verse? What is the original word for "soul"? (Hint: We learned it in the previous chapter.)

B. What do you see people trading their soul for in this world? What about girls in your own age group? What do they trade their souls and personalities for?

C. Create an expression board. Get a stiff piece of cardboard. On one side of the cardboard, show the person you are on the outside. You can use colors, pictures from magazines, rubber bands, paperclips, flowers, whatever you want!

DAY 5
Read Psalm 103:15-17

A. What are our days like? According to this verse, how are we like flowers? What lasts forever?

B. What things about you are going to fade and pass away? What things about you will last for eternity?

C. Get the expression board you created yesterday. As we learned in these verses, what is inside of us is the only thing that will last. Yesterday you created who you are on the outside. Today, flip your expression board over and create who you are on the inside.

CHAPTER 3

Why Am I the Potato?

For You formed my inward parts;
You covered me in my mother's womb.
I will praise You, for I am fearfully and wonderfully made,
Marvelous are Your works, and that my soul knows very well.

PSALM 139:13-14

A Chapter on Comparison

The Potato Complex

If you've ever sat in a group of friends and wondered why some people get all the good looks…

If you've ever looked in the mirror and your first thought was, "Yuck…"

If you've ever wanted her hair, those eyelashes, or that reason for a training bra, you, my friend, have experienced the Potato Complex.

The Potato Complex is a theorized condition rampant around the world. It is most common in women and usually develops in the pre-teen years. I know all of these impressive facts because…well…I made it up. Like any girl, I had my lapses of Potato Complex, but I didn't have a name for it until thumbing through my Instagram one day. A middle school girl in my newsfeed had posted a model-esque picture of herself, and she looked fabulous, perfect hair, perfect body, stunning smile. Of course, the comments were all the same. "SO GORGEOUS!" "Giiiiirrrrrl, *fire emoji, fire emoji, fire emoji*"

Then there was one comment, one that stood out from the others. This comment came from a real-live middle school girl who'd had enough. "How come you like that, and I still look like a potato?!"

And thus, the Potato Complex was born. There are women who live their entire lives battling the Potato Complex. The Potato Complex is not limited to outward appearances. Oh, it starts there. Round about the age of twelve, we start looking around us at our peers and realize that if we're going to fit in and feel attractive, we need to "look more like her." But that's just the early onset of the Potato Complex. It reaches new heights in high school when we're not only pressured to "look like her" but also to "have a boyfriend like her" and "be popular like her." If we're not careful we will live the rest of our lives comparing ourselves to that successful career woman, that perfect wife, and that Pinterest-worthy mom. We need to deal with our Potato Complex, and we need to deal with it now.

Stop Trying to Be Her

Whether we're talking about models, selfies in our social media feed, or the girls in our class, it's easy to get caught up in comparison. At Bible study, we might not admit it. We don't want to come across as shallow, but when we're just with our friends, it's a different story. Before long we feel that little, green-eyed monster creep its way in. Things start to slip into our speech, things like, "She's so pretty it's not even fair!" or "I wish I looked like her." or *groans like walrus* "GOALS!"

Hate to be the crusher of Pinteresty dreams and the soul-sucker of Insta-goals, but darling, you are never going to look like her. Not now. Not ever. Know why? Because you're not her, and you were never meant to be her. We spend so much time looking at other girls' gifts', talents, and waistlines that we lose sight of our own significance.

Quick pop quiz! Name a few of the ten commandments. What are the first ones that come to mind? The first ones mentioned are usually the "big ones," like don't murder, don't steal, and don't bow down to idols.

The tenth commandment is one we don't think about very often.

> *You shall not covet your neighbor's house;*
> *You shall not covet your neighbor's wife,*
> *Nor his male servant, nor his female servant*
> *Nor his ox, nor his donkey, nor anything*
> *That is your neighbor's.*
> Exodus 20:17

Not many of us are tempted to covet our neighbor's donkey. So how can this verse possibly apply to us?

Every sin of humanity begins with the sin of coveting (wanting what you don't have). We do it on an hourly basis. If we didn't covet, we wouldn't have bad attitudes, unkind thoughts, or cruel words. For ancient Israel, those things were different. If their neighbor had the latest model of the iPhone, they probably wouldn't have cared. That donkey tho!

For us, the struggles are still real, but different.

If the tenth commandment was written for middle school girls today, it would probably read,

"Thou shalt not covet your neighbor's good looks;
Thou shalt not covet your neighbor's male admirers;
Nor her Instagram followers, nor her huge group of friends,
Nor her perfect hair, nor her perfect skin,
Nor anything else that is your neighbor's."

Hits a little closer to home, doesn't it?

We were not meant to waste our lives wishing that we were somebody else. Trust me, that girl has plenty of her own problems to deal with. She doesn't show it. She doesn't talk about them. They never make it to her Instagram Story, but her life bears struggles and scars that you cannot imagine.

While we do often covet the outward appearance of our neighbor, we also covet the internal strengths.

We want to be smart like her.

We want to be funny like her.

We want to sweet, bold, adventurous, and liked...like her.

All of these character traits are wonderful things to want, but if we're envious of our friends who have these qualities, it's still coveting. It will still make us discontent, and leave us disappointed.

Finding "You"

The five of us sprawled on the beach blankets. We were high school seniors, about to launch into our futures and desperate for some summer fun. The bean dip had been devoured. The stories had been told. The sun was disappearing behind the horizon. It was time for some honest girl talk.

"Skinny jeans…are not my thing," one of my friends confessed with the utmost gravity. "They don't look good on me. They have never looked good on me. The other day I realized that they probably never will." She stared up at the sky with an expression of relief. "And I've never felt so free."

"I can't tan," another girl confessed. "It doesn't matter how hard I try. I sunburn. I will always sunburn, and I just realized…that's okay."

"My hair is crazy thin," I admitted, twisting it into a tiny little knot. "It will never be glorious, flowing locks. It will always be short. It will always be thin. For the first time in my life, I'm okay with that."

I remember that conversation so vividly, the moment that each one of us realized that we didn't have to be what the fashion magazines said. Just because a certain style was popular didn't mean that it was right for us, and for the first time, that was okay. For the first time, each of us felt comfortable in our own skin. Because all our lives we'd felt insecure about our body types.

This world wants you to feel insecure. Not only that, it is trying to make money off of your insecurity.

This world wants you to buy makeup that will hide your gorgeous freckles, jeans that will disguise your natural curviness, and accessories that will make you feel "good enough." This world wants you to constantly compare yourself with photoshopped models and fake women. Do not be trapped by chains of comparison.

You were fearfully and wonderfully made, and if God saw fit to give you that hair, that shoesize, or that waistline, then, girl, you rock that look! Do not let this shallow world tell you who to be and how to look.

Insecurity is a lifestyle. If we're going to break free of it, we need to change how we look at ourselves. We need to see the beautiful creation of God when we look in the mirror. I've seen girls who even think that insecurity is a form of humility. That is not true.

Despite what One Direction may have led you to believe, smiling at the ground and being ashamed of how you look, *does not* make you beautiful. It makes you insecure.

You know what's beautiful? Confidence. I don't mean arrogance. Nobody wants to hang out with a girl who thinks she's better than everybody else. Everybody wants to hang out with a girl who isn't ashamed of who God made her to be.

A girl who finds her God-given confidence does not need to prove herself.

A girl who finds her confidence doesn't have to follow after what everyone else is doing, saying, or wearing.

A girl who finds her confidence finds her own style and rocks it.

A girl who finds her confidence doesn't need to show off her body to get boys' attention or make other girls jealous.

A girl who finds her confidence is the type of girl that others follow and look up to.

A girl who finds her confidence will light up the world like nobody else.

She knows that physical beauty will fade. She knows that the spark God placed inside of her is something this world needs. She knows that her God has given her beauty for ashes. You are the precious possession of the Living God who calls you beloved, chosen, and masterpiece. That, beloved girl, is what makes you beautiful.

CHAPTER 3

Why Am I the Potato?
Daily Study Guide

DAY 1
Read 1 Peter 3:3-4

A. According to these verses where shouldn't we find our worth? What fashion trends are most beautiful to the Lord, according to verse 4?

B. What does incorruptible beauty look like in the people around you? Can you think of someone who exemplifies a gentle and quiet spirit?

C. If you were to develop a fashion line of beautiful, inner qualities, what would it look like? Would they be bold, bright colors? Soft, subtle lines? Sketch out your fashion line this week, drawing clothing that represents the qualities that you want in the closet of your heart.

DAY 2

Read Exodus 20:17

A. What does it mean to covet? What seven things are we told not to covet?

B. Make a list of the things you are most tempted to covet? What do you envy that other people have?

C. Pray over that list you made. Each of us have areas where we fall into habits of coveting and envy, but we can be free of them when we confess them to our Savior.

DAY 3

Read Psalm 90:16-17

A. What four things does this prayer ask for? What do you think it means to let "the beauty of our God be upon us"?

B. This verse clearly connects beauty with hard work. Why do you think that is? What does the beauty of the Lord have to do with the work of our hands?

C. What work has God put into your hands today? What tasks are still before you this week? Pray over them, asking God to make your hard work count and bring Him glory.

DAY 4

Read Isaiah 61:3

A. What three trades does God promise to make with His people in this passage?

B. How has the Lord given you personally, beauty for ashes? Just like we saw in Psalm 90, when our beauty comes from the Lord, it is established. When we are able to find our beauty in Him rather than the world's standard, we're able to stand confidently, "like trees of righteousness." How does these things make us confident?

C. This week, be on the lookout for people who are struggling. Everyone has their own ashes, mourning, and heaviness that they battle with. When you see someone who is suffering this week, encourage them with reminders of the beauty, joy, and praise that can be found in Jesus.

DAY 5

Read Ephesians 2:8-10

A. What are we, according to verse 8? Why were we created?

B. Have you ever accomplished something or created something that took a lot of work? Maybe you won an important game or poured your soul into a piece of art or a poem. The word for "workmanship" in this verse means "masterpiece" or "poetry." That is what God sees when He looks at you.

C. Be prepared to share about your "masterpiece" with your Bible study group. Describe what work went into it, and how you felt when it was finished.

CHAPTER 4

No Filter

Do not let your beauty be merely outward,
—arranging the hair, wearing gold,
Or putting on fine apparel—
Rather let it be the hidden person of the heart,
With the incorruptible beauty of a gentle and quiet spirit
Which is very precious in the sight of God.

1 PETER 3:3-4

A Chapter on Authenticity

Social Butterflies

You are stranded on a desert island. You have one banana, enough clean water for one day, and a band-aid. Rescue is unlikely. You may be trapped here for the rest of your life, and you can only take...one...photo filter.

Which one do you pick?

Think about it! One filter for the rest of your life. Which one do you choose?

Would you go for a soft, Instagram option to really bring out the bruise in that banana?

Or maybe you'd pick the beloved Snapchat Puppy Face. That won't get old after a few decades, right?

I don't mean to bring you down by asking you such a life and death question. Hope I haven't killed the mood at Bible study.

In our generation, this is a very prevalent question that must be considered carefully from all points.

Which filter would bring out the best starvation selfie?

Which filter would accurately capture everything from puddles of stagnant water, to oceanic sunsets, to desert island vlogs?

How would we live without our filters? Don't get me wrong. I have nothing against phot filters. They're fun!

But imagine if you used only one for the rest of your life, if every picture you posted was a Face Swap with the nearest, abandoned volleyball or a Black and White of the monkey that stole your band-aid. It would get pretty old pretty quickly.

Social media is one of the biggest topics of middle school. Which one is the most popular? How many follows does it take to feel like valued member of society? And—most importantly—when are you old enough to have it?

Maybe you're the social media queen.

Maybe you're still waiting for the day when you can hashtag with the best of them, but either way, it's a huge part of the world we live in. What exactly is a filter?

If you were to look up this word in the dictionary, here's what you would find:

Filter

noun | fil·ter | ˈfiltər

(def.) A device used to strain out unwanted material

From the filter that removes the nastiness from our drinking water to the photo filter that hides the pimple on our chin, this is their primary purpose. Different filters remove different unwanted materials that we don't want others to see.

We use filters on our personalities too.

Just like a rosy glow on an Instagram photo or a fake

face on Snapchat, the filters that we use in real life hide the qualities that we don't want other people to see. These filters help us to hide our fears, insecurities, and doubts.

Middle school is the time when we're deciding how we want people to view us. As we're building up who we are and who we want to be, we need to watch out for these three personality filters that might just strain out the most authentic parts of us.

Filter #1: Puking Rainbows

We all love this one, don't we? Open your mouth and what comes out? Joy, happiness, and rainbows. What could be better?

However, in real life, this filter looks a little different. The girl who uses this personality filter is honestly a little scary in person. Conversations with her usually look like this:

Rainbow Puker: Hi! How was your day?

You: It was good. How was yours?

Puker: My day was AMAZING! I mean, I just LOVE LIFE so much!!! Omigosh. Look at all these texts. I'm so busy. It's not easy being this popular. *People*! Why are you so obsessed with me? This weekend I had…like…three birthday parties to go to, and I had to decide which one to go to and it was really hard.

And so on, and so forth until you leave the conversation feeling like the most unpopular person to ever walk the earth.

What She's Filtering Out: At first the rainbow puker might just seem like a really positive person. Positivity is a good thing, but this girl doesn't want you to see who she truly is.

She covers up her struggles, problems, and true self with a bucket load of gloppy rainbows. Her end goal is to have the kind of life that other people look at and envy. She rarely opens up, because on the inside, her life is anything but rainbows. Often times, rainbow pukers also feel the need to filter out the silence and therefore talk at every opportunity. They surround themselves with noise and people so that they never have to face themselves in the mirror and question who they really are.

Her Biggest Fear: The Rainbow Puker lives in fear that someone will look her in the eye and ask, "How are you, really?" I once had a rainbow puker in a Bible study I taught. She laughed off every question and when asked what struggles she faced, she responded, "I don't like questions like that," and refused to answer. The thing is, rainbow pukers aren't usually driven by anger or even self-centeredness as they might appear. Rainbow pukers are driven by fear, fear of being truly known. They fear that if anyone truly knew who they were, they wouldn't have any friends.

What God Says to Rainbow Pukers: God is not fooled by the rainbows we spit up. He knows our deepest difficulties and fears. He is pleased when we open our mouths in truth and love and light, but true delight is found in Him, not in popularity or circumstances. He has seen all of us at our worst, but while we were still sinners (and rainbow pukers) Christ died for us (Romans 8:28). He isn't afraid of the side of us that no one else sees. He wants to fill us with a joy so deep that we can throw that filter aside and be who we truly are.

Filter #2: Frowny Face

What's more fun than Grumpy Cat memes? Looking like Grumpy Cat. We all have our Frowny Face days, but some of us hide in the Frowny Face on a regular basis. This is not only unpleasant, but it's a dangerous place to be. The Frowny Face starts out as a ploy for attention. When you ask Frowny Face how she's doing she responds with a sigh and a shake of her head. She's tired. She's "Okay, I guess." She's the opposite of the Rainbow Puker. She's never happy. She wouldn't be happy if she won a million bucks. Why? Because Frowny Face thrives on other people asking, "Are you okay?"

Let me make something perfectly clear. I am not talking about someone who is fighting the very real battle of depression. I'm talking about the person who wears a fake attitude for the sake of getting attention. Frowny Face isn't struggling with true depression. Frowny Face actually has a pretty amazing life, great parents, and friends that care about her. She just wants attention for being depressed. However, if she isn't careful, her lack of thankfulness will lead to real depression in her teens and young adult years.

What She's Filtering Out: Frowny Face is filtering out the people who care most. She likes the idea of being the only one standing against the world. If she were to write her autobiography it would read, "No one believed in me. I was all alone." That's how she views life no matter how many people love and support her. She likes to see herself as the struggling soul. The truth is, she is surrounded by people who love her, and her entire slump could be solved with an extra dose of thankfulness.

Her Biggest Fear: Frowny Face's biggest fear is that she will eventually push everyone away and be truly alone. Sadly, this is often a self-fulfilling fear. She's so afraid of pushing people away, that she never lets them in to begin with. She sits in the back of the church and pouts, then wonders why no one talks to her. She shows up to youth group and puts other people down, then says that she doesn't feel included. At heart, this girl is afraid that people don't really care about her, and is willing to shove them all away to prove it.

What God Says to Frowny Face: Jesus promises this girl, just like He promises all of us, "I will never leave you, nor forsake you." (Hebrews 13:5) Her worst fear will never come to pass with the Lord. However, if she rejects His help the same way she rejects the blessings He's already given her, she will dig herself into a hole. Jesus once came across a Frowny Face in His ministry. The man was a cripple, who had stayed by the pool of healing for years. When Jesus met this man, He didn't say, "Oh no. You poor thing. What happened? Tell me all about it." He asked him one simple question. "Do you want to be healed?" Jesus asks Frowny Face the same question. Do you want to be a healed, whole person? Do you want to be happy? Because it's possible! He has promised us a fulfilling life of joy, but if we try so hard to filter out the blessings, we will miss that life entirely.

Filter #3: Face Warp

When it comes to selfies and short videos, this is my favorite filter. Transforming you like the mirror of a fun house, this filter twists and contorts your face until you hardly recognize yourself. In real life, the Face Warp filter can be a dangerous thing. It's got a lot of fancy words like "self-deprecation," but at the end of the day, it simply means that Face Warp Girl thinks she's not good enough. She looks in the mirror and sees a twisted, contorted version of the gorgeous girl that God created. Rather than cover herself in makeup and an artificial social life (like the Rainbow Puker would) she constantly insults herself. Not just her looks, but her personality too. She's the girl who hates herself in photos. She's the girl who is always making comments like, "I'm horrible at this." In truth, she's often fishing for compliments to boost her self-esteem. If she walks around talking about how awful she is, someone is bound to come along and say, "No, you're not. You're beautiful and talented." But when they do, it doesn't fix the problem, and Face Warp Girl still feels horrible about herself.

What She's Filtering Out: Face Warp Girl has convinced herself that she is ugly, untalented, and unlikeable. However, instead of trying to hide behind other people, Face Warp Girl filters out every positive comment and encouragement. She talks herself out of any confidence she could have had. Whenever someone gives her a compliment, her first response is, "No, I'm not."

Her Biggest Fear: Face Warp Girl is a perfectionist. She holds up an impossible standard to herself and then wonders why she never feels good enough. Her biggest fear is that she will never measure up. She will warp, twist, and bend over backwards to be good enough, interesting enough, and worthy of everybody's love, including God's.

What God Says to Face Warp: Jesus didn't come for the

perfect. Which is good, because if He had, Heaven would be empty. He came for the lost, the hurt, the broken, and the warped. We are all messed up sinners. Our hearts are all warped. Realizing this is the first step to repentance and forgiveness. However, we were never meant to live lives of shame or talk down the creation made by the hands of God. We were created to live boldly. Romans 8 says that we are free from "condemnation." That's a big word for the creepy-crawly feeling in our stomachs that tells us that we are not good enough. None of us are worthy of God's love! But in Him, we have been given beauty for ashes (Isaiah 61:3) and can live in freedom.

Footloose and Filter Free

1 Peter 1:3-4 says not to let our adornment be merely outward. This is usually applied to our makeup, jewelry, and clothing, but in this generation our outward adornment can also be filters and Photoshop.

You and I were never meant to experience life through a filter. We were meant to be all that Christ intended for us. We were meant to let the hidden person of our heart shine through unashamedly. He didn't die for us so that we could live life depressed, stressed out, or wishing we were someone else. He knows us, truly knows us, and He loves us despite our flaws. It's time to let go of our filters and live the life of freedom we were meant to live.

CHAPTER 4

No Filter
Daily Study Guide

DAY 1

Read 1 Peter 1:7

    A. What is our faith compared to? What three things is it meant to do?

    B. Have you ever met someone who was genuine? To be genuine means to be honest, raw, and real in what we believe. The Lord has put people in our lives to be Godly examples of what authenticity and genuine faith looks like. Prepare to share with your group who your role model of genuineness is.

    C. Make a list of ways that the genuineness of your faith and your personality could bring praise, honor, and glory to the Lord.

DAY 2

Read 2 Peter 1:5

A. What are we supposed to give? What two things are we supposed to add to our faith? What do these two words mean?

B. In the list of ways to grow our character, we're to add these things first. How can you add these things to your faith this week?

C. Ask God to reveal one new thing about Himself to you today. Once you've asked Him, open His Word and let Him increase your knowledge of Who He is.

DAY 3

Read 2 Peter 1:6

A. What two things are we told to add to our faith? Which one do you feel is the easiest to add? Which one sounds the hardest to add?

B. What areas in your life are hardest to persevere in? Is there anywhere that you struggle with self-control?

C. Take away one thing from yourself today. It can be anything, television, social media, dessert. Exercise your self-control in this one area as a test to see how much self-control you have.

DAY 4

Read 2 Peter 1:7

A. What two things are we to add to our faith from this verse? Why are these the most important things?

B. Who in your life is hardest to be kind to? Who is difficult to love?

C. Do one random, secret act of kindness today to practice brotherly kindness and love. You can clean something for your mom without being asked or give up some of your time to play with a younger sibling. Whatever you do, do it secretly, and make sure you don't get caught!

DAY 5
Read 2 Peter 1:8

A. What promise is given to us in this verse? What will we gain if these character traits are ours?

B. Have you ever seen someone who embodies these qualities of genuine faith? Who are they? What do you learn from them?

C. If we possess the qualities that we've been studying this week, we will not lack any good thing. We will not have the need of a filter. We will be free to be who we truly are. This week your youth leader can post a picture of your group with no filter using the hashtag #justusgirlsstudy to share what the Lord has showed you this week.

CHAPTER 5

When He Doesn't Like You Back

That Christ may dwell in your hearts through faith;
That you, being rooted and grounded in love,
May be able to comprehend with all the saints
What is the width and length and depth and height—
To know the love of Christ which passes knowledge…

EPHESIANS 3:18-19

*A Chapter on Boys, Crushes,
And What to Do About Them*

Where the Lie Begins

Our group had grown up together, gone to Sunday school together, and now, approaching our teen years, we spent the evening splashing in the pool as our parents chatted inside. We laughed and joked back and forth as the night went on. It felt wonderful to let go of all the arguments that had separated us as kids and have fun. Boys no longer had cooties. In fact, they were funny, and pretty cute. All things considered, this was the best thing I'd done all summer.

I thought we were having a great time.

Apparently, not everyone felt the same.

Halfway through the night, one of the older boys leaned over to my brother and whispered, "Man, your sister is so annoying. Why is she even here?"

I cried for days.

I'd heard a lot of insults. I'd been called stuck up, a

buzz-kill, and a horrible friend. I was able to separate those comments. I knew they were false, but this was my worst fear come true. As a middle schooler, I lived in terror that my friends secretly found me annoying. My biggest social struggle was silencing the lie that no one even wanted me around. Now, that lie had a teenage boy's voice.

It played in my head all throughout middle school.

I took it with me into high school. Soon I forgot who'd even said it. It had become so ingrained in my thinking. I would see a boy that I liked and consider talking to him, but I would stop myself. After all, I was annoying. He wouldn't want to talk to me. Why even try?

This lie took root in my mind, sprouted, and grew branches of insecurity.

I was annoying.

I was unattractive.

Guys didn't want me around.

I didn't know how to talk to guys.

It wasn't until I was in my twenties that I realized what a monster of insecurity I had. In my young adult years, I met incredible brothers in Christ who talked to me, laughed at my jokes, and never called me annoying.

I'd believed a lie for years. All because of an immature comment from a teenage boy, who—I guarantee you— doesn't even remember it.

It doesn't matter if it's a boy we like, a boy at our school, or just the bully that grew up down the street from us. The kid who let that comment fly at me over the chlorine wasn't even my crush. He was just some random boy.

And his opinion mattered.

In middle school, what boys think starts to matter to us. Which is unfortunate because middle school boys say a lot of stupid things. Things that they don't remember, don't understand, and don't even mean to say.

If we're not careful, they will mess with us. If we're not careful, the effects can last for years. If we're not careful, middle school will be the beginning of an avalanche of self-doubt.

Sticks, Stones, and Broken Bones

Let me start off by saying something that has shocked middle school girls all over the world: You are not too young to like a boy. It is completely natural, normal, and acceptable for you to notice boys and find them attractive. I say this because I've heard adults tell middle school girls that they shouldn't even be thinking about boys at their age. That's just not true. You shouldn't be *acting* on these feelings, but having them is part of life and it's nothing to be ashamed of. You are a girl. You were created to be loved and cherished. That doesn't mean that you should head out your front door at this moment and find a boy to chase. Like I said, these feelings aren't meant to be fulfilled at this time in your life. Overthinking them leads to unhealthy thought patterns and wrong priorities. Your life is supposed to be about so much more than just boys right now. You are becoming a young woman. You are discovering who you are. You are finding your confidence. Don't lose sight of all that for a boy.

Now I do not want to start a man-hating rant. It breaks my heart when girls get together and have a little pity party.

"Girl, where are all the good men?!"

"We don't need them. We've got chocolate!"

That is not what this time is for. Boys are no better or worse than girls. They simply are. They're flawed humans, just like us, and they say stupid things, just like us. All the same, we need pull ourselves together and find our confidence before the off-hand comment of the nearest cute guy ruins our day.

Believe me, that guy is *going* to ruin your day at some point. He is *going* to say something offensive. At some point in your middle school experience, you are *going* to be mocked, teased, or in some way degraded by the very people you are trying to attract.

And it's going to sting.

You might cry for days.

You might wake up in your twenties and realize that what he said still bothers you.

So how do we prevent this? How do we find our confidence when the boys around us don't like us back, or worse, make us feel ugly and unwanted?

The first key is to gain a little insight into the puzzle that is middle school boys.

Many of you may remember from elementary school that most classic of courtships, that most elegant of romantic moments, the playground fight. We've all seen it, the little boy who wants to meet a little girl and win her heart. He therefore proceeds to call her names, shove her out of trees, and throw comparatively large objects in her general vicinity.

Moms have a word or two to say on the subject. Usually something to the effect of, "Oh, he just did that because he secretly likes you." Adjusting the ice pack on your branch-shaped bruise, you—like me—probably didn't believe her, but she was right. By the time we hit our pre-teens nothing much has changed. In middle school, we've simply traded in our rocks and sticks for sarcasm and insults. This goes both ways. We're not exactly peachy to the boys we like. We often let insults fly without thinking, because we're trying to be funny or catch their attention.

Being on the receiving end of this process hurts like crazy. But it's very true that the boys who are meanest to us sometimes just want to catch our attention.

Much Love

I remember watching a movie with my little brother years ago. The guy-gets-girl happy ending was fast approaching, and I felt it my sisterly duty to warn the four-year-old that the lovey-dovey stuff was coming up. "You'd better close your eyes," I cautioned. "They're gonna kiss."

I dared a glance in his direction.

He stared placidly at the screen, eyes-wide, smile huge as hero kissed heroine.

"What's with you?" I asked, dumbfounded by his enjoyment of my favorite princess movie.

He grinned up at me and shrugged. "I love, love."

We're girls, and let's face it. We love, love. As we should.

> *That Christ may dwell in your hearts through faith;*
> *That you, being rooted and grounded in love,*
> *May be able to comprehend with all the saints*
> *What is the width and length and depth and height—*
> *To know the love of Christ which passes knowledge...*
> Ephesians 3:18-19

We were meant to be rooted and grounded in love. We are meant to stand our ground and dig our roots deep into the love of Christ.

Our job in this lifetime is to try to understand the

dimensions of God's unmeasurable love for us.

The width. A love that would cross any distance to get to you.

The length. A love that is impossible to outrun.

The depth. A love that we can lose ourselves in completely.

The height. A love that is not contained by any precaution or restraint.

If we truly take in what it means to be loved, the knowledge of Jesus Christ's perfect love for us will cast out any fear of the rejection (1 John 4:18). We were not meant to live in the fear of what boys think of us, but in the confidence of what our God says to us.

Rise up, my love, my fair one
And come away.
For lo, the winter is past,
The rain is over and gone
Song of Solomon 2:10-12

CHAPTER 5

When He Doesn't Like You Back
Daily Study Guide

DAY 1
Read Ephesians 3:17

A. How does Christ dwell in our hearts? What two words does Paul use to describe our relationship to God's love?

B. Have you ever seen a large tree that wasn't deeply rooted? What happens? Our lives might grow and flourish above the surface. We might be popular, and even have the attention of all the boys we know, but if we are not rooted in God's love, our lives are going to come crashing down. How can you tell if someone is firmly rooted in God's love?

C. If your life was a tree, what would it look like? In your journal, draw a picture of a tree. Label the branches with what goes on in your life above the surface. School, friends, etc. Then label the roots. What are you rooted and grounded in? What holds you together and keeps you steady?

DAY 2
Read Ephesians 3:18

A. What are the four dimensions of God's love? Here's the crazy thing, in our physical world, there are only three dimensions. Why do you think that God's love gets four?

B. How wide is God's love? How long is it? How tall is it? How deep is it?

C. Get a ruler or a measuring tape and measure a small object, a book or a box. What is its length, width, and depth? Now, using your ruler or measuring tape, go measure the ocean. (I'm just kidding. You don't really have to measure a massive body of water.) Measuring God's love in one lifetime is as impossible as measure the Pacific with a ruler. However, there are practical ways that we learn more about the love of God. Share about a time when you learned something new about God's love.

DAY 3
Read Ephesians 3:19

A. What are we supposed to know? What are we supposed to be filled with?

B. Have you ever had a moment when you felt God's love overflowing you? Maybe it was in a quiet moment with just you and Him. Maybe it was when He helped you to show love to someone when you didn't want to. Describe this time, and be ready to share it with your group.

C. Spend time in prayer, asking God to give you knowledge of His love and to fill you with all the fullness of Himself.

DAY 4

Read Ephesians 3:20

A. What is God able to do? How is able to do it, according to this verse?

B. The entire purpose of this passage is that God's love for us is so great that we could never understand it. Have you ever seen God do something that was better than you ever imagined?

C. Okay. Time to dream big. Imagine yourself in ten years. What is the best life you could possible imagine? Discuss your dream house, dream guy, and dream life. Be prepared to share this with your group. Whatever your God has planned, it's exceedingly abundantly above whatever you imagined just now. Your future, your life, and your love story is in God's hands. Prepare to let Him blow your mind.

DAY 5

Read Psalm 91:14-16

A. Why does the Lord promise to deliver you in this passage? What does He promise to do? When will He be with you?

B. The deepest longings we have cannot be fulfilled by people. That crush of ours will never love us the way that our Savior does. Do you want a hero who will arrive to rescue you, set you on high and love you endlessly? You've got one. Jesus' love will never be a disappointment. Look up one woman of the Bible and describe how God loved her, delivered her, and was with her in trouble.

C. Discuss a time when the Lord rescued you from trouble like your knight in shining armor and set you on high.

CHAPTER 6

Eeny-Meeny-Miny-No

The righteous should choose his friends carefully,
For the way of the wicked leads them astray.

PROVERBS 12:26

A Chapter on Choosing Your Friends

A Golden Revelation

I'd heard about life flashing before one's eyes in moments of peril but hadn't expected to experience it just yet. After all, I was only five.

My playmate had wanted to play "Puppy." After announcing this, she had tied one end of a red doggy leash to the doorknob and the other end around my neck. Seeing that her work was done, she promptly left me to suffer my fate. Now, on the verge of certain death, I looked back over the many time I'd gotten myself into these horrible situations and decided then and there that if I survived this ordeal, I needed to make some changes to my life. Being five years old, I hadn't had many moments of introspective revelation, but the time had come for me to take back my life.

The first order of business would be to remove the "Manipulate Me" sign that was surely taped to my backside. It must have been there for years. How else could I explain all of the terrible ways my friends had controlled me throughout my Kindergarten experience?

First, there had been the "Mermaid Incident." My best friend had informed me that a mermaid had come to live in her backyard. Being a clever, realistic child, I gave it thirty solid seconds of consideration before I bought it hook, line, and sinker.

Then there was the "Birthday Incident." A friend wanted to play Barbies. I wanted to play hide-and-seek. I was adamant. I would not be moved. She gave a disappointed shrug. "That's fine, I guess. I just...I thought that you wanted to come to my birthday, and if we don't play what I want to play, you can't come." Horrified at this threat of social homicide, I allowed myself to be blackmailed for the better part of Kindergarten by this clever tactic. Later, in the older, wiser months of first grade I came to find out that this child didn't even know when her birthday was, nor did she ever have a party.

Those experiences had been unpleasant, but this—*this*— took the cake.

Here I sat, alone in my room, about to be strangled by a dog leash. What a way to go. The game "Puppy" had sounded so harmless. Urged on by the words, "Your mom doesn't need to know. It'll be fun!" I'd given in so easily.

I now saw the game for what it was, but too late. My fate was as tightly sealed as the knots securing me to the door. I'd never seen a six-year-old tie such knots.

There I sat, quite calmly wondering if I would suffocate before my "friend" came back. In the meantime, I looked back over the many experiences that had landed me in places like this. It was there, tied to the door knob that I stumbled upon a glorious revelation: "I need better friends."

Luckily, my mother noticed my absence and came to my rescue. I was released from my strangulation. Needless to say, the companionship with said playmate ended rather abruptly that day. Cutting ties was preferable to being forcibly drowned in my cereal on the next playdate.

Perhaps it was that day that drove the lesson home for me. Because that is the last time that I can remember being manipulated into a dangerous situation by a friend. Oh, that doesn't mean that all my relationships were golden. There were plenty of fall outs, BFF breakups, and high school hardships ahead of me. However, the "Doggy Leash Incident" taught me a lesson that wove itself permanently into my brain. In grade school, middle school, and high school, peer pressure didn't affect me as much as it could have.

Every time one of my friends would start out with, "Your mom doesn't need to know. It'll be fun!" My memories would start giving me a lecture.

It sounds fun now, but you know where it's going to end? With you tied to a door.

This memory made it much easier to tell my friends, "Y'know what? I'm good. You guys go ahead."

I think that lots of girls could have saved themselves years of heartache and peer-pressured drama if they could've spent five, reflective minutes tied to a door as a child. That one incident changed the way I viewed good friends, bad friends, and what to do about them.

Dodgeball

Many of us dreaded the fateful words on the playground, "Pick your teams."

Deep inside, so many of us fear being the last one picked, not just in dodgeball, but in life.

We don't want to be the unpopular kid. We don't want to be the last one picked.

How can we be absolutely sure that we will never be the uncool kid? How can we know that we won't be the last one picked?

Simple. Be the one doing the picking.

As we enter the complicated social construction that is middle school, life is presented to us as a game of chance.

You'd better hope that the right friends choose you. You'd better hope that you're cool enough to sit with them, hang out with them, and be one of them.

This places such immense pressure on us that it can distort our confidence until we don't know what happened to the bright, bold thing we used to be in third grade.

We're so afraid of being alone, of being unliked or unnoticed.

Girls who think like this in middle school set themselves up for a world of heartache in the future. If you don't learn how to pick a good friend in middle school, you will not know how to pick a good boyfriend later on. This passive attitude in our relationships can lead to an adulthood of insecurity and a mindset of unworthiness.

> *The righteous should choose his friends carefully*
> *For the way of the wicked leads them astray.*
> Proverbs 12:26

If we want friends worth having, we need to start doing the picking. So get up off that bench. You and I are going to go friend shopping.

The Perfect Fit

Whenever I talk to girls about finding the right guy, I tell them to make a list of things that they want in a husband. This is a great exercise that shows exactly what kind of guy you want and keeps you from getting distracted by guys that are not what you're looking for. We want to pick the right guy, don't we? Someday, we want a guy who cares about us, treats us with respect, loves God (and hopefully super hero movies). By the time we're thirteen, some of us know exactly what we're looking for in a guy.

And yet we leave our other relationships to chance. Most of us believe that God has a plan for our love lives, but we treat friendships like they just "happen." Then we wonder why so many of our relationships are drama-filled and unhealthy. We need to make a list of things that we are looking for in a friend. Each of us is different. Some of us want a friend who wants to face the great outdoors together. Some of us want a friend who will come over and watch Netlfix with us and discuss our favorite books. These are the optional items on our list. But what about the core list? What are some qualities that should be on everybody's friendship list?

1. Someone who encourages. This might seem obvious. Wouldn't we naturally be drawn to people who encourage us? Yes, but in middle school, it's all too easy to confuse compliments with encouragements. Someone who follows you around telling you how great you are, isn't necessarily an encourager. They could very well be a person given to flattery. When we pick our friends, we need to be searching for people who encourage others on a daily basis. Lots of

relationships can be based off of negative things, like envy, gossip, and complaining. Soon the friendship is nothing more than a pity party. Eventually, friends like that are going to need something new to complain about, and they're going to pick you. You want someone who is kind, helpful, and encouraging, not just to you, but to everyone. Pay attention. How does your friend treat their parents, their teachers, their siblings? That's who they really are. Even if they're nice to you, that unkind side of them is going to turn on you at some point. Search for someone who does things without complaining and without arguing (Philippians 2:14).

2. Someone who likes the real you. A manipulative friend will always try to change you. When we think about this, we usually think, "I would never let someone change me." But they can be subtle about it. It usually comes out when you relax, unwind, and start to be yourself. They usually have a sarcastic comment like, "Oh my gosh. What are you doing?" They will make you feel small and embarrassed about the things you love. They will criticize your taste in music, your dance moves, and your family. If they were blatant about it, we wouldn't put up with it, but it creeps in. I'm not talking about a horrible person. I'm talking about a sweet girl that everybody loves who says things like, "Are you really going to wear that?" and "Stop it. You're embarrassing me." These things are usually said in joking, but quickly eat away at our confidence.

3. Someone who is low drama. Some people are just drama magnets. They end up in horrible situations with horrible people, and expect you to bail them out. Run. Do not walk. Just run. You need to separate yourself from the

drama. Sometimes that means separating yourself from people who are in the middle of it. The middle school question of the hour is, "Shouldn't I be there for my friends?" If they're trying to drag you into their ugly, miserable situation, girl, they are not your friends.

A perverse man sows strife,
And a whisperer separates the best of friends.
Proverbs 16:28

Taking Inventory

Think of your three closest friends. Do they fit these criteria? If they don't, you need to consider taking a step back. Should you drop them like a hot potato, and say things like, "I've decided not to be friends with you."? No, but you need to emotionally step back from people who do not lead you in the direction that you want to go. There are always going to be people in our lives who take from us more than they give. These people are our ministry. We can show them the love of Jesus. We can be a good friend to them, but they are not meant to be our nearest and dearest kindred spirits. Save that special place for people who encourage you to be better, love you for who you are, and draw you closer to Jesus.

It can be painful to take that step back. Sometimes the people who are the most unhealthy are the friends we've known since childhood. We put up with their drama, their antics, and their manipulation. Why? Because we've known them since birth! However, the fact that they're childhood friends does not necessarily make them good people. Case in point, one of my childhood friend tried to strangle me with a dog leash.

In middle school, we sometimes believe that there are two kinds of people in the world, our closest friends and everybody else.

That is not how we were created.

We were meant to have a wide range of relationships. We were not meant to be best friends with the whole world. Throughout your life you will have classmates, roommates, co-workers, and friends that are not what you're looking for in a good friend. Don't feel bad about holding these people at a distance. There is nothing wrong with protecting your heart. Authenticity and openness are important in our close relationships, but they are not for the whole world.

A fool vents all his feelings
But a wise man holds them back
Proverbs 29:11

Your thoughts and feelings are precious. Do not set yourself up for heartbreak by sharing them with people who are not going to appreciate or understand them. This world is full of wonderful, fascinating people who are going to encourage you, value you, and be a steady influence in your life. Don't miss out on them because of the drama-makers. Sometimes we miss these amazing people because we're not looking in the right places. Are you short on friends? Have you looked inside your own family? Sometimes our own parents or siblings are off our radar because they are so close to us. Sometimes our closest friends can be kids younger than us, or even adults in our church. We are meant to have a wide range of relationships. If you have trouble finding good friends, start thinking outside the box.

The key to separating good relationships to not-so-good

relationships is simple—keep Jesus in the center of your heart. If Jesus is our center, the axis on which our whole world turns, we will not be shaken by the worst storms of any friendship.

Eeny-Meeny-Miny-No
Daily Study Guide

DAY 1
Read Proverbs 12:26

A. What should the righteous do? Why?

B. What are some of the best friends you've ever chosen? Why?

C. Make a list of qualities you are looking for in a good friend. Do you know anyone with these qualities? (Don't forget people in your family and people who aren't in your age group.)

DAY 2
Read Proverbs 16:28

A. What does a perverse man do? What does a whisperer do?

B. Have you ever had a friendship destroyed by a whisperer or a misunderstanding? Have you tried to make it right?

C. Pray over that friend and the situation and, if possible, try to make peace with that friend.

DAY 3
Read Proverbs 29:11

A. What does a fool do? What does a wise man do?

B. Do you agree with this? Why do you think venting your feelings is foolish? Do you have rough time holding them back? Why, or why not?

C. On a separate piece of paper draw a small circle at the center, a wide ring around that, and an even wider circle around that one. Write Jesus at the center of your circles. In the middle circle, write the names of the kindred spirits whom you trust and would tell anything to. In the outer circle, write the names of people whom you like and see on a regular basis, but don't necessarily count as close friends. This graph isn't for anyone but yourself. You need to decide who your deepest, closest relationships are. Are you working on those relationships and helping them to thrive?

DAY 4
Read Proverbs 27:6

A. What will a friend give you? What will an enemy give you?

B. Have you ever had an enemy that multiplied compliments? Have you ever multiplied compliments to get on someone's good side?

C. Share about a time when you received an honest wound from a friend. How did it help you?

Day 5

Read Proverbs 17:1

A. What two kinds of meals are described in this verse? Which one is better? Why?

B. Have you ever been at a feast (or a dinner table) where there was strife?

C. Drama, drama, drama! What's a girl to do? Sometimes we feel powerless against drama (what the Bible calls "strife"). Have you ever had to step back from a drama-filled situation?

CHAPTER 7

What Brave Girls Do

For You are my rock and my fortress;
Therefore, for Your name's sake,
Lead me and guide me.

PSALM 31:3

A Chapter on Bullying

Spill It

He waited on the playground, the spare change in his palm, gathering sweat. Enough spare change to buy him a lollipop at the gas station down the road. But this change wasn't meant for lollipops. No, it had a much more exciting purpose. He waited until the younger kids wandered into the play area. "Hey!" He called to one of younger boys. "Do you want a quarter?"

Delighted at this sudden upturn in his fortune, the little boy nodded eagerly.

The older boy smiled, took a quarter in his hand, and proceeded to pitch it at the younger kid as hard as he could. *Thwack!* The quarter hit the kid's arm, leaving a perfectly round, red mark. Stunned, the little boy stared in shock at the forming welt. The bully laughed, and the kid ran in fear of being attacked by further riches.

The boy with the change continued to wait in his corner of the playground. Some children cried. Others picked up the coins and hurled them back in his direction. Like many other eight-year-olds that day, I was struck by a quarter from an impressive distance, I stared the kid down, picked up my well-earned quarter, and slipped it in my pocket. *What a jerk*, I thought, moving on with my play time.

I was rarely bullied as a child. I have tried many times to understand why that was. Lots of my childhood friends experienced it, and—as the quarter incident clearly demonstrates—they existed. However, neither myself nor my brothers were bullied as children. We had the occasional name-calling problem or quarter incident, but for the most part, we stayed out of such dramas. As I considered why, I realized that it had little to do with the bully in question. It had everything to do with what I did next. Or rather, what my family did.

Growing up in my house was like growing up a house of overly invested detectives. We have a sixth sense when it comes to secrets.

Most families might ask, "How was your day?"

And then there's my family. "How was your day? How did you do on your test? Oh, good. I'm glad it was a good day. Was it *really* a good day? Or was it really a bad day, and you don't want to talk about it? Because I noted that you're walking a little slow and making 15% less eye contact than a typical Thursday afternoon. Also, you're home exactly three-and-a-half minutes earlier than usual. Did something happen at practice? Was someone mean to you? DO YOU HAVE AN EMPTY SPACE IN YOUR HEART?!?!?!"

See what I mean? My home was where secrets went to die. They didn't have a chance.

My parents weren't control freaks, but they cared so deeply about us kids that I seriously pity the people who ever meant us harm.

That night as I ate dinner with my parents, they gave each of us kids the typical, "How was your day?" interrogation. The quarter story came spilling out. My mom gave me a reassuring hug and the classic, "He just does those things because he has a crush on you," speech. My dad, however, took a different approach. He said little at the dinner table, but on my next visit to the playground, he sent me to play. I'd long forgotten the quarter incident by then, and ran off with several friends. My father spotted the bully looking cool on the edge of the playground. He walked up behind him. "Hey kid," he called, waiting for the boy to turn around.

"What?"

My dad smiled. "Want a quarter?"

The bully (who was actually just a terrified, ten-year-old kid) dissolved into a puddle of apologies.

The quarter-hurling career ended then and there. There was no drama. No parental sit-down. No continued bullying.

Why? Because when we were teased, we had someone to talk to. I had a mom who was ready to listen, and a dad who could make any grade school bully wet their pants. Granted, my parents also had a healthy dose of, "Dust yourself off and deal with it." They didn't come in guns-a-blazing for every playground infraction, but on several occasions, they stepped in. Talking to them saved me bullying, drama, and situations that I couldn't handle by myself.

When to Call in the Cavalry

None of us want to be the tattle-tale, the snitch, the squealer. When should we dust ourselves off and deal with it? And when is it time to blow the whistle? Believe it or not, there is actually a Biblical guideline for this found in Matthew Chapter 18.

Moreover, if your brother sins against you,
Go and tell him his fault between you and him alone.
If he hears you, you have gained your brother
Matthew 18:15

We've all said and done mean things without meaning to. Often, much of the behavior people refer to as "bullying" really isn't bullying at all. It's some friendly joking that went too far. It still hurts feelings and still divides friends. However, it is not a reason for you to go to your teachers and report that you've been bullied. If your friend offends you or hurts your feelings, the Bible is clear. Tell them. They might not even know that their teasing hurts you. Hopefully, they will apologize, and you will gain your friend back. However, some people will not hear you.

But if he will not hear,
Take with you one or two more,
That 'by the mouth of two or three
Witnesses every word may be established.'
Matthew 18:16

Here's what this *does not* mean: Go form a girl gang and go after the bully. This is EXACTLY the kind of drama you should avoid at all cost. Your two or three witnesses should be your parents. If you've told this person that you've been hurt, and they will not hear you, go to your parents, and let them give you guidance on what to do next. If their involvement doesn't solve thing, then it might be time to inform the powers that be (the school, the bully's parents, etc.).

If there is a dangerous situation, and you think that someone might get hurt, don't wait to have a heart-to-heart with the bully in question. Find the nearest adult.

Monopoly Theology

Have you ever played a good, old-fashioned game of Monopoly? I don't mean the new one with credit cards where you buy McDonalds. I mean classic Monopoly. With the boardwalk and the little houses and the shoe. The idea of this game is to buy property with your Monopoly money. Simple, right? Until you draw the Jail Card. This card sends you directly to jail with no benefits. You cannot pass GO. You cannot collect your $200. You go straight to the clink.

Middle school sometimes feels like a board game. We're the shiny little shoe moving our way around the board, and sometimes scary situations land in our lap out of the blue, like the Jail Card. What should we do?

Do not pass GO.

Do not collect $200.

Go DIRECTLY to your parents.

What do we do when our friend shares a secret that could hurt them, or someone else?

Do not pass GO.

Do not collect $200.

Go DIRECTLY to your parents.

Secrets that seem harmless in middle school can lead to ugly, dangerous situations. If you feel that one of your friends is in danger, you need to be a good friend to her. A good friend doesn't keep secrets that could hurt people. A good friend informs a safe adult and saves their friend from further harm.

What if someone corners us and threatens us?

Do not pass GO.

Do not collect $200.

Go DIRECTLY to your parents.

"But I don't want to be a tattle-tale." Bullies love to tell you you're a tattle-tale. It's a tactic of manipulation. If there is a kid who has threatened you in any way, it's time to tell your parents. Sadly, kids aren't the only ones who use this tactic. I once had an adult lose their temper and scream and yell at me. After their temper tantrum they told me, "Don't tell your parents this ever happened." Guess what I did?

I didn't pass GO.

I didn't collect $200.

I went to my parents.

Keeping quiet doesn't make you brave. It makes you a vulnerable target to bullies in the future. Having open lines of communication between you and the adults that God has placed in your life will save you so much heartache and drama. Informing a parent, a teacher, or an adult you trust, will save, not just you, but countless other kids from being victims.

What if we get into a terrible situation that we know could get us into trouble, and we don't know how to get out? (Say it with me.)

Do not pass GO.

Do not collect $200.

Go DIRECTLY to your parents.

Trust me. Even if you're afraid of getting in trouble, there is a freedom found only in honesty.

Of course, there are exceptions. Maybe you don't live with your parents. Maybe your parents genuinely don't want to hear and don't want to help. In these cases, you need to find a Godly adult, like a youth leader or a pastor who is going to be there for you and help you make the tough calls.

So often in middle school we feel the pressure to be grown up and handle things. We put ourselves in situations that adults wouldn't touch with a ten-foot pole. It's not a question of whether or not you can handle it. It's a question of whether or not you want to be neck deep in drama.

Do you want to be weighed down by the burdens of other people?

Do you want drama to follow you everywhere you go?

Do you want your life to be the subject of gossip and the target of bullying?

No. None of us should want a life like that.

Take refuge in the safety of the authority that God placed in your life. Being mature or grown up does not mean that you take on life all by yourself. We all need each other. We were never meant to be alone in this world. God gave you a family in the Body of Christ.

All of us want to be brave girls, as we should, but there is some confusion as to what a brave girl does when faced with a bully.

If there is someone manipulating you, if there is someone who is out to destroy your confidence, if there is someone bullying you into silence, speak up. Take a stand. You do not have to put up with behavior like that. If it is possible to make peace, or to simply separate yourself, do it. If not, don't be afraid to tell the adults who love you what is going on. It is not a sign that you are weak. It does not make you less of a warrior. Bullies are nothing more than cowards.

They are cruel manipulators that are afraid of brave people like you. Don't fall into the trap that so many others have. Take a stand against the bullies, the cowards, and the cruel people of the world. Your Heavenly Father has blessed you and will deliver you. Take advantage of the Godly people He has placed in your life. Reach out for help.

Because that is what brave girls do.

What Brave Girls Do
Daily Study Guide

DAY 1

Read Matthew 18:15-16

A. What are you supposed to do when there is a problem between you and a friend? What are you supposed to do if they don't listen?

B. Have you ever seen a friendship mended by an apology? What did that restoration look like? Are there any relationships in your life now that could use healing and restoration?

C. Is there someone that you've had a conflict with? Someone that you need to talk to? Go to them this week, in love, and restore that relationship. Make things right, and gain your friend back.

DAY 2

Read Psalm 34:4-6

A. What happened when David sought the Lord? What happened when he cried out?

B. Are there areas or people in your life that are giving you trouble? Have you ever cried out to God in the midst of your troubles? What happened?

C. Pray over an area of your life where you need the Lord to deliver you. It could be an outward problem like bullying, or it could be an inward problem like fear. Pray these verse over your situation and ask for God's deliverance.

DAY 3

Read Psalm 31:1-5

A. What names does David use for God in this passage? What does he ask God to do?

B. If anyone knew what it was like to be manipulated and bullied, it was King David. He worked under King Saul, a classic bully. Both Psalm 31 and Psalm 34 are written by David when he was being oppressed and bullied. What do you think it means when it says that God is our fortress?

C. Share about a difficult time in your life when God was your fortress and your refuge.

DAY 4

Read James 1:26-27

A. What kind religion does a person have if they can't control their own tongue? What does pure and undefiled religion look like?

B. Maybe you're not the type of person who is bullied very often, but what can you do to keep others from being bullied? The Word of God says that we are to show kindness to the oppressed and to stand for what is right. Have you ever been in a situation when you had to stand up for something and someone? What happened?

C. Do something unselfish this week. These verses show us what true Christianity looks like. Though we might struggle here and there with other people's unkindness, there are people in the world who truly are oppressed. Find someone to show kindness to. Is there an elderly person you can help for a day? Is there a mission organization you could give money to? Think big.

DAY 5
Read John 8:31-32

A. What shows people that we are Christ's disciples? What sets us free?

B. Has the Devil ever lied to you or bullied you? He tries to bully all of God's children, but our Heavenly Father will not stand for that. He has given us the weapon of His Word. What lies has the Enemy told you?

C. The ultimate bully is the Devil. He bullies us with all sort of lies and half-truths. The only way to overcome his bullying is by standing on the truth of God's word. Write down three truths from the Bible that destroy the lies that the Enemy tells you.

CHAPTER 8

You Lost Me

Ask, and it shall be given to you
Seek and you will find;
Knock, and the door will be open to you.
For everyone who asks receives,
And he who seeks finds,
And to him who knocks it will be opened.

MATHEW 7:7-8

A Chapter on Facing the Future

Simple, Right?

Have you ever been lost?

I have. Many times, but I remember one in particular.

I'd only been in the little Scottish town two or three days, when my wonderful host asked me to drop by the church that afternoon. All I had to do was walk to the church from her house. That's it. Over the next several months, I got to know that walk so well that I could have done it in my sleep. That first time, however, I asked her to explain it to me no less than three times.

"Walk to the end of the street. Take a right. Walk on that street to the highway. Take a left."

Simple, right? Her directions were punctuated with phrases like, "It's right around the corner," and "There's no way you can miss it."

Guess who managed to miss it? This girl.

I wandered the Scottish streets for nearly an hour. No

reception. No Google maps. I was a helpless, jetlagged, Millennial.

I had to stop and ask for directions multiple times. I was on the verge of tears trying to find this place.

I could have kissed the nice lady with the stroller who finally pointed me in the right direction.

I stumbled onto the church's walkway like a ship-wrecked sailor onto dry land. FINALLY! I had reached my destination. Nobody else had been there to witness my blunder (except that nice lady with the stroller). I decided then and there that I would never tell a soul how lost I had been on such a simple journey.

I tell you this story in the utmost secrecy. To this day no one in the church knows how the poor American missionary wandered the streets of Scotland. I trust that my secret is quite safe with you.

In middle school, our futures hold so much. High school, driver's licenses, and our teen years are right around the corner.

Simple, right?

Getting there is a different story.

If we're not careful, we can end up lost on our way to the future, struggling and wandering and embarrassed.

Watch Me

After that day, I learned to give myself lots of extra time before stumbling my way through a new environment, allowing myself to get my bearings. I've learned never to trust the words, "You can't miss it," or "There's no way you could ever get lost."

Watch me. I promise you, if there is a way to get lost, I

will find it. If there's not a way to get lost, I'll invent one.

Have you ever gotten lost on your way to the future? Have you ever looked around you at the friends you have or the person you've become and wondered, "How did I get here?"

On our way to the future, all of us get a little bit lost. We all get lost for different reasons, but especially in middle school it's all too easy to lose your sense of direction in the midst of the chaos and the hormones and the struggles.

Some of us get lost because we're not paying attention. We get distracted along the way. The squabbles and struggles of middle school become our whole life. I'm not talking about the big things. I'm talking about the little things that we won't even think about in five years. I'm talking about the drama, the arguments, the "he said, she said" that draws us away from the Lord, and our healthy relationships.

Some of us get lost because we rush. We charge forward. We don't want to be twelve. We want to be fifteen. So we find friends who are several years older. We talk like them, dress like them, and act like them. We treat other girls our age like dirt because we want to be one of the older, cooler kids. However, rushing doesn't get us to our destination. Maturity cannot be learned overnight. God has us on a step-by-step, day-by-day journey. When we try to rush, we end up in places we never meant to be. I know high school looks fun, but trust me, God has you in middle school for a reason. Trust Him with His timing.

Some of us get lost because we've got the wrong address. This happened to me just the other day. I was meeting someone at a house I'd never been to. They told me the street name, and I typed the address into my phone. I arrived at my destination right on time, only to realize that

I'd typed in the wrong street name and ended up on the other side of town. Sometimes we feel lost because we're heading for the wrong address. We want to be liked more than we want to please God. We want to be rich and famous more than we want His guidance. These are the dead-end streets that lead us nowhere.

Some of us get lost because we lose our focus. You always aim toward what you focus on. I remember learning this firsthand the day I got my training wheels off. I decided to go careening down a hill, when I noticed my little brother nearby. I was worried about crashing into him, that I focused on him. Because I was focused on him, my handle bars turned that direction. So did my wheels, until I nearly collided with him. Our life goals are no different. We might say that we want to be Godly, confident young women in ten years. But if we're not focusing on the Lord and being a confident young woman now, we'll never reach our true destination.

Some of us get lost because we took a wrong turn. I remember watching a TV show where contestants were in a race for a million dollars. They had to search a large city for their next clue. Most of the teams found the clue quickly, but one team took a wrong turn. They got so turned around that they eventually were disqualified. The thing is, it wasn't the wrong turn that lost them the race. It was the fact that they wouldn't admit they were wrong. They insisted that they knew where they were going and drove for hours in the wrong direction. In Hebrews 12 Paul says that our faith is a race. In our race, we all make mistakes. We all get off track. We all lose our way and wonder where we went wrong. Our mistakes will not hurt us nearly as much as our pride. In the Gospels, Jesus was compassionate to people who had made horrible mistakes. He showed them love, grace, and mercy. The only people that Jesus was hard on were the self-righteous who would never admit their mistake. James Chapter 4 tells us that God resists the proud, but gives grace to the humble. The word for "resist" means to hold at a distance or to strong-arm. Lucky for every one of us, God doesn't resist the sinners. He doesn't resist the lost. He doesn't resist the people who make mistakes, but He *does* resist those who will not admit it. If you and I take a wrong turn, develop that attitude, say something we regret, or just head in a direction that we know isn't right, we need to be willing to admit when we are wrong. We need to stop and accept that we are lost, and we need to admit it by turning around and finding our way back.

Just Ask!

Whether we are rushing, distracted, or just flat-out wrong, once we realize that we are lost, we need to find our way back to where we started. If we keep peddling in our wrong direction we're just going to get even more lost.

This is a problem I see so often among teens and young adults. They wander around wondering, "What does God want me to do?!" Often, the reason they can't figure it out is that they didn't do the last thing God told them to do.

If you and I find ourselves wandering and lost, we need to go back to the basics. We need to remember Jesus' love for us. We need to remember that He is our Way, our Truth, and our Life. Even if we think we're on course, we need to reassess our hearts now and then. Little missteps right now can result in big mistakes later. Little course corrections right now will save us from huge heartache later.

Feeling like you're never pretty enough now can result in a self-loathing problem.

Retreating deep into yourself when you're upset can result in depression.

Chasing boys might seem harmless now, but when you're older it will result in the breaking of your heart.

When we do get lost, all it takes is one step, one cry, one prayer to get back to the Lord.

Ask, and it shall be given to you;
Seek and you will find;
Knock, and the door will be open to you.
For everyone who asks receives,
And he who seeks finds,
And to him who knocks it will be opened.
Mathew 7:7-8

Jesus will withhold no good thing from the girl who asks. That's all it takes, just like my pathetic self, begging directions off of that mommy with the stroller. That promise isn't just for those of us who feel lost. Even if you are walking in step with the Lord right now, there are areas of your life where you need direction, where you need wisdom. You're starting to make decisions about your life, about who you are and who you want to be. Sometimes we feel like these decisions are too trivial to take to the Lord, but He cares about the smallest details of our lives.

If any of you lacks wisdom,
Let him ask of God, who gives to all
Liberally and without reproach,
And it will be given to him.

But let him ask in faith, with no doubting,
For he who doubts is like a wave of the sea
Driven and tossed by the wind.
James 1:5-6

God wants to be the desire of our hearts. He wants to be our everything. He wants to give us the direction we are looking for. If we never ask Him for wisdom, we will end up driven and tossed by the wind. We will be blown off course by every new idea, every distraction, and every mistake. We'll take scary turns down some dark alleys of insecurity and selfishness. All we need to do to keep from getting lost is ask.

In our spiritual walk, we need to be willing to be honest about where we've gotten lost. Not just with God, but also with our Christian brothers and sisters. It's painful to discuss the times we've messed up and gotten lost. It takes a huge dose of humility, but it can save us. If we're willing to share with that friend, that youth leader, or that parent, that we are struggling, they can help us back to where we need to be. If we're willing to share where we've gotten lost, it can also save the lives of others. Not only that, but we get to see the Lord use our past difficulties and mistakes. We need to be vulnerable enough to say, "I got lost. I didn't know where to go. I needed to find my way back to God, but He brought me back." That can save other from those same pitfalls.

Do not fear, sweet girl. You and I are going to make it home to Heaven in one piece, and we are going to have some stories. Just stick with your God. He knows where you're headed, and He will get you safely home.

CHAPTER 8

You Lost Me
Daily Study Guide

DAY 1
Read 1 Thessalonians 5:8

A. What are the children of the day supposed to be? What are supposed to put on?

B. The word for "sober" here means clear-headed. We are supposed to have clear heads, not full of distractions as we pursue God with all we've got. Have you ever seen someone pursue God like this, without distraction?

C. Make a list of the things that distract you from fully following God. All of us have those things in our lives. Sometimes that list is full of fears and doubts. Sometimes it's made up of more practical things, like social media. Write out your list and give it up to the Lord, asking Him to keep you from temptation.

DAY 2
Read Philippians 4:11-13

A. What six situations does Paul list? What did they teach him?

B. Being discontent with this season of your life isn't going to help you in your journey to the future. Of all the situations that Paul listed, which one do you feel like you're in right now? What is it teaching you?

C. Share about two times in your life when you had plenty (we could be talking about things, friends, or anything that made you feel good about life). Share about a time when you didn't have much at all. How did these times teach you contentment?

DAY 3
Read 1 Corinthians 9:24-27

A. What picture is described in these verses? What are we told to do? What is a sin?

B. The word "sin" is actually an archery term. It means "to miss your target." As a Christian young woman, what is your target? What are you actively doing to reach that target? What could throw you off?

C. What do you need to change in your life in order to hit your target?

DAY 4
Read 1 John 1:9

A. What are we told to do in this verse? What happens when we do it?

B. Is there anything in your life that you need to ask God's forgiveness for? If nothing comes to mind, think a little harder. We've all got areas of unconfessed in in our lives. We need the courage to bring it before God.

C. Pray for God's forgiveness over these areas of your life, freely admit the places where you have messed up, and be set free by His glorious forgiveness.

DAY 5
Read Romans 12:5-6

A. What picture do these verses paint? What does it mean to be the Body of Christ?

B. We were given to one another to bear each other's burdens and share in each other's weaknesses. Don't be afraid to share your mistakes and mess ups with the brothers and sisters in Christ all around you. We are family. We were meant to encourage and lift each other up. Have you ever seen Christian brother and sisters help one another in a time of crisis?

C. Think of a time when you got off track in your walk of faith, and be prepared to share it with your Bible study group, or a Christian leader who is close to you.

CHAPTER 9

Drive Me Crazy

A fool vents all his feelings,
But a wise man holds them back.

PROVERBS 29:11

A Chapter on Controlling Your Emotions

Your First Driving Lesson

"I don't know. A Ferrari, I guess," I finally offered.

"Seriously?" My younger brother gave me a pitying look.

"What's wrong with a Ferrari?"

"It's so basic," he groaned. "Everyone wants a Ferrari."

"Fine," I huffed. "What's *your* dream car?"

"A black Lamborghini Centenario Roadster."

Okay. When it comes to cars, I'm basic. I'm not into cars. If I can afford it, and it gets me from point A to point B without breaking, it's my dream car. However, this doesn't cut it with the average fourteen-year-old male.

Do you have a dream car? Is it about the style and the color? Or is it all about the power? If money was no object, what car would you buy?

I actually find myself laughing through car commercials from time to time. Sometimes I like to mute the commercial and narrate it myself.

"See this guy? His name is Bloated Jo. He used to be sad and dumpy like you. Then he got a car. Now he knows where he's going. Now he has abs. Now girls talk to him. Our latest model is everything you need in life. Beautiful. Powerful. Dangerous. Buy our car. Be like Jo."

In middle school, we dream of the day when we can sit behind the wheel of a car. You might not be ready to take the wheel of a real car just yet, but that doesn't mean I can't give you your first driving lesson right here in bible study. That's right. Buckle yourself in, girlie. I'm going to give you a driving lesson right here, right now. Because our emotions have the ability to take us places, and if we don't plant our booty in the driver's seat now, we might just run off the road. Let's take a spin with our beautiful, powerful, dangerous emotions.

Get to Know Your Vehicle

Our emotions are simply our reactions to circumstances, attitudes, or other people. They can feel good or bad. It depends on the emotion we're discussing.

Some people hate emotions and would rather toss them out altogether. They don't want to feel pain, so they choose not to feel at all. When we choose not to feel, we miss out on exhilaration, joy, accomplishment, compassion, empathy, anticipation, and all the other feelings that make us human.

Other people live by their emotions. They follow the advice of Disney songs and follow their heart wherever it leads. The problem is, if we let our emotions run the show, we're going crash.

Before we get behind the wheel and learn to use the powerful tools that God gave us, we need to take a good look at them. What is an emotion? What is a feeling? Is it a good thing? Is it a bad thing?

The answer is, it's neither. Feelings aren't good. Feelings aren't bad. They just are. We can't discredit them. They make up who you are and how you respond to people and to life, but we can't fully trust them either. Our hearts are deceitful and desperately wicked (Jeremiah 17:9), and not even we can know the depths of them.

Each person's set of emotions is different. Some of us have enough energy and excitement to drive a freight train. Some of our tempers go zero to sixty in 2.5 seconds. Some of us get weepy at any moment and our emotions leak all over the place.

What would you say is your biggest emotional struggle?

Getting to know your emotional response to the world is one of the most important things any girl can do in middle school. Because guess what? These emotions are a part of you. They're not going anywhere. Learning to control them is a scary, wobbly process. There may be times when your parents fear for their lives and hit the brakes.

We need to learn to control them before they control us. Hop in!

The Emergency Break

"Now let's get one thing straight," my Driver's Ed teacher announced from the front of the noisy classroom. "We are *not* going to call it an emergency brake. If we call it that, then we'll only use it in case of emergencies. It is a 'Parking Brake,' and you should use it every time you park your car."

An emergency break can save your life. If you can't picture what it looks like, it's that lever or handle that the driver pulls when they park on a hill. It usually makes a huge cranking sound when they pull it, and it keeps you from rolling away into traffic and certain death.

Everyone needs a mental emergency break. It can be employed in a number of emotional situations.

When you really want to let that person have it, hit the brakes! You'll regret losing your temper on that friend, that sibling, or that parent.

When you just can't stop thinking about that guy, and you know you really shouldn't be thinking about it…but just a few more minutes of day-dreaming, hit the brakes! Getting lost in a romantic fantasy will leave you in a state of discontentment and frustration.

Just like my Driver's Ed teacher warned us, there is a danger in saving your emergency brake for emergencies only. Sometimes we save it for last.

We think that we can take control of our emotions in a worst-case scenario.

We hold a grudge against someone, thinking we've got it under control, until they push our buttons. Then it all comes gushing out.

So many girls have fallen into the trap of believing that they can flirt and play with teen romance. Playing with fire and giving into those emotions and fantasies will cause us to forget about the brakes entirely.

We need to learn to pull our mental emergency brake early on.

For the weapons of our warfare are not carnal,
But mighty in God for…bringing every thought into captivity
To the obedience of Christ.
1 Corinthians 10:4, 5

We need to take our thoughts, even the tiny ones, captive before the hurt us. We need to learn to use our emotional brakes before we lose control of the car. Don't just reserve that emotional control for the emergencies. Use it on a regular basis.

The Security System

I learned to drive in a gray Jeep Cherokee the size of a boat. We drove that faithful car for years, before it finally gave up the ghost. In one of its last stages of life, our Jeep (we called it Jeepers) had a total nervous breakdown. There is no other way to describe what happened to it.

One day I was driving it down a friend's steep driveway, and it snapped. I lost all ability to steer, my brakes stopped working, and the entire car died in the middle of the driveway. Luckily, I knew where to find my emergency brake, but it was months before we were able to get the car fixed.

One of the key problems with the car was its security system. This particular car had an anti-theft setting to keep the car from being stolen. If anyone tried to steal the car, it would shut down and die. Somehow on the sunny day I had been driving it, the car had decided that it was being pilfered, and it panicked. In short, Jeepers had an irrational fear of being stolen, which led to a nervous breakdown.

Our security system defines what we fear most. Our worries and fears, irrational and rational alike cannot be allowed to control us. Why did the car shut down? Because it didn't feel safe. This world is a scary place. Often in middle school, we're realizing that for the first time. And if we base our safety and our security on our circumstances, we will freak out and shut down. The only thing that will help us to overcome these fears is to know that our safety, our comfort, and our security lies in the Savior who overcame this scary world. If we truly learn to trust in Him we will save ourselves a lot of freak outs, and maybe even a nervous breakdown or two.

Low Gear

I live at the bottom of a hill. A crazy, scary, steep hill. A mile of straight up and down. The first time I drove it, I was terrified, but before long, the hill became good, clean fun. The only problem with a hill like this one, is that if you don't use the brakes, you could crash.

You should use the brakes, like we talked about, right? Wrong. Using the brakes on a hill this steep will fry them. Instead you use something called low gear. This causes the car to slow itself down and go down the hill without you losing control or killing your brakes.

The feelings we experience in middle school are new and exciting, even the weird ones. We've never felt this much before. We've never understood things this deeply. Even our outbursts and meltdowns are accompanied by a depth of feeling we've never experienced, and in a weird way, it's fun.

As we test our new emotional dimensions, we love to throw ourselves into things.

We don't just get a little weepy. We have a good ugly cry.

We don't just get a little upset with the situation. We're ready to start throwing punches.

We don't just think about that cute guy sometimes. We think about him whenever we have five seconds, and sometimes even when we don't have five seconds and our teacher catches us and asks us what we're thinking about and now we're just embarrassed.

Teens and pre-teens alike are known for their explosive emotions and they're all-or-nothing view of life.

Do we need to engage the brake? Yes, but if we engage the brake every single time we feel something, we're going to burn out.

Instead, we need to learn to approach things carefully. Rather than rushing into a situation swimming with drama, we need to put our minds and our hearts into low gear and approach these situations carefully. It's okay to be excited. It's okay to be sad. It's even okay to be angry, but rushing headlong into a situation like this will get us into trouble and cause us to say and do things we will regret. Just like we learned back in Chapter 6...

> *A fool vents all his feelings,*
> *But a wise man holds them back.*
> Proverbs 29:11

The Rear View

It's okay if this stuff doesn't come naturally. Driving is hard. Driving your emotions? That's a lifelong lesson. Just one last driving tip before we pull back into the drive way. Don't forget to check your mirrors. They are there to help you with your blind spots.

All of us have blind spots, struggles and flaws that we can't even see. Looking back at where we've been, and the emotional mistakes we've made in the past, will help us to overcome them.

Some people never learn from their mistakes and live a

life defined by their emotions. You and I were called to live abundant lives.

Our emotions are beautiful when used for the purpose God intended.

We were meant to find excitement in life.

We were meant to relate to other people.

We were told to weep with those who weep and rejoice with those who rejoice.

We were meant to be angry and not sin.

We were meant to enjoy these emotions, not to be controlled by them.

It's time to take the wheel, dear one. We've got places to be.

Drive me Crazy
Daily Study Guide

DAY 1
Read Psalm 139:15-16

A. When did God first see us? When did He plan out our days?

B. What is your biggest emotional struggle? Why is it difficult for you? God crafted you to be uniquely you. You might have a hot temper. You might cry easily. You might think that there is something wrong with you, but God created those emotions for a special purpose, if we can learn to harness them.

C. What practical things can you do to control this emotional struggle? What tools has God equipped you with to help you?

DAY 2

Read 2 Corinthians 10:3-5

    A. What are our weapons good for?

    B. What thoughts are hardest for you to take captive? Why?

    C. Create a practical plan in your journal for when these thoughts creep into your mind. What are you going to do? What verses are going to strengthen you?

DAY 3

Read 2 Timothy 1:7

    A. What hasn't God given us? What has He given us?

    B. The words for "sound mind" can also mean self-control. Sometimes our emotions make us feel like we're losing our minds, but that is not the life that God created us to live. What does it look like when someone walks in the three qualities that the Lord has given us?

    C. Pray over the fears in your life. Give your worries over to God. He has given you a sound mind of self-control, and you can beat this thing, sweet girl.

DAY 4

Read Proverbs 29:20

    A. What two people are described? Which one has more hope of success in life?

    B. Proverbs has lots of negative things to say about foolish people, but not even foolishness is worse than a person who can't keep their mouth shut. Describe a time when you were hasty in your words and regretted it.

    C. We can't always predict the times when we'll be tempted to be hasty in our words, but sometimes we know when we're heading into situations that will tempt us to say things we'll regret. Do you have any situations like this coming up in the next week? Pray over them, and ask a Godly leader to pray for you.

DAY 5
Read Proverbs 24:16

A. What is a righteous man's life plan?

B. The righteous fall and make mistakes, but the difference between the person who succeeds and fails is the person continues to get back up and learns from their mistakes. What areas of your life do you need to get back up and try again?

C. Share about a time when you learned from a mistake.

CHAPTER 10

Outside In

The King's daughter is all glorious within:
Her clothing is wrought of gold.

PSALM 45:13 KJV

A Chapter on True Beauty

Fit for a Queen

Seven-hundred-and-seventy-five rooms.

Forty-thousand light bulbs.

Three-hundred-and-eighty-four years old.

I stood at the gates of Buckingham Palace, enthralled.

In America, we have no concept of royalty. True, we have DC and the oval office. However, a palace puts our democratic grandeur in perspective. Buckingham Palace is an experience even from the outside, standing outside the gates to see the guards on parade, but my day didn't end there. Not only did I get to see the gold crested gates and endless windows.

I got to go inside.

I got to view the carriages, the paintings, and the state rooms. I got to wander the halls where some of the greatest men and women in history have danced, dined, and laughed. I stood in the throne room and saw the thrones of the monarchs. I got to see the finest clothing of the country's longest reigning monarch.

My eyes didn't pop back into my head for at least three days. My jaw muscles were sore from all the gaping. I'd never seen anything like it in my life. The ceilings went on forever. The gardens sprawled in every direction. Most of the furniture was older than my country.

This was the palace that little girls dreamed about.

It was a day I will never forget. It doesn't matter if I'm on the busy city streets, or cramped in a small apartment. My heart has a secret. I've been to the palace. I've hobbed with all the knobs that once knobbed around those worth hobbing with. I've stood in the throne room. I've seen the royal table set and prepared for the guests.

And no one will ever take that away from me.

If you were queen of the world. If you could have a palace of your very own, what would it look like?

Would there be turrets? Towers? Would you spend your days exploring hidden rooms and coaxing secrets from the furniture? Would you want a modern palace? Or a medieval castle? Would there be a swimming pool? A movie theater?

Well, it just so happens that I know an Architect who might be willing to take on the project. He has great experience building mansions, and even whole cities (John 14:2, Hebrews 11:10). He has set out to create something beautiful—not just in jolly old London town—but in your heart.

A Fixer Upper

If I asked you to tell me about your home and your family, what would you say? You'd probably tell me about your parents, your siblings, what you like about them, maybe some favorite family memories.

Here's what you wouldn't say: "Yellow. Blue roof. Lots of windows."

Why? Because you wouldn't be describing your home. You'd be describing your house.

Middle school is the first time when we start thinking about our "earthly house." What coat of paint do we want people to see? What is the most important thing about us? What kind of house do we want to be? Are we going to be the tough girl, the smart girl, the girly girl?

I love picking paint colors. It's one of my favorite things. I love repainting rooms and interior decorating. It's fun! Likewise, figuring out what kind of person you want to be is one of the best parts of middle school. However, if we're not careful, we can become so obsessed with the outside, that we start to believe that's all there is.

What if Buckingham palace was only nice from the outside? What if it was a dump on the inside? What if there was garbage everywhere? What if Prince Phillip's socks were on the dining room table? What if Lizzy's knickers were on the floor?!

I—for one—would be disappointed.

2 Corinthians 5 calls our bodies our "clothing" or our "earthly house." It's our outside, our personality, the things we are good at or interested in. Paul warned the Corinthian church that our outside—our "earthly house"—isn't going to last. Our interests, skills, and talents are going morphs as we get older. Our earthly house changes over time. This is one of the more painful parts of growing up. Even in middle school, we can look back and see that we're not the same person that we were five years ago. We've changed, and

sometimes that change is painful. Paul knew this.

> *For we who are in this tent groan,*
> *Being burdened, not because we want to be unclothed*
> *But further clothed, that mortality may be*
> *Swallowed up by life.*
> 2 Corinthians 5:4

Okay. There are a lot of big, Bible words in there. What this verse is saying is that we can't hold on to the temporary things in this world. Our looks, our talents, the things we take pride in are not going to last. This is a painful, scary realization.

If your achievements, your talents, and your persona were all taken away, what would be left?

We can't hold onto our persona, our "clothing." And it's not that our "clothing" is a bad thing. The reason the verse says that we groan is because you and I long for something deeper. We don't just want to be a beautiful palace from the outside. We want to be the individual that God created us to be. We want all of these games and social cliques to be swallowed up by the beauty that Jesus offers us.

No Place Like Home

Have you ever been afraid to let people in? Afraid to show them who you truly are on the inside? It's easy to hide behind the social life. It's easy to fix up the outside of a house. Remodeling the inside is a different story. Cleaning up the inside of our hearts intimidates us. We'd have to clear out the drains of unforgiveness and show grace to people. We'd have to rewire our reactions to be kind to others. We'd have to knock down some bitter walls and get elbow deep in some bad habits. That sounds like a lot of work, but if we spend all our time perfecting our outsides, we will never be the confident young women we were created to be.

Your outside is exactly what God made it to be. You are already beautiful on the outside. The God that formed you chose your hair color and put each of your eyelashes in place. He created you with particular talents and interests.

Are you listening? *Really?* If you're not, dial in right here, right now. Because this is the key. This is what will make you a confident girl right now, in middle school.

Let the outside be, and let your God build a palace within your heart.

There are plenty of girls who are pretty on the outside. Just like there are plenty of pretty buildings in Europe. What makes Buckingham Palace special is not its size or its beauty. It's special because of who lives there.

Don't be the girl who's just pretty on the outside. Be the girl who has endless rooms full of grace in her heart. Be the girl whose heart is worth visiting. Be the girl that people look at and say, "God must live there."

So we are always confident,
Knowing that while we are at home in the body,
We are absent from the Lord
For we walk by faith, not by sight.
We are confident, yes, well pleased rather
To be absent from the body and to be present with the Lord.
2 Corinthians 5:6-8

Do you want to be the confident girl who has nothing to fear? Do you want to rest securely in who you are?

Confidence in your personality, in your social life, and in your appearance, will never get you through this life.

Confidence is found when we realize that these things are temporary. Our looks, our likes, they're all going to change. Realizing that those things are temporary decorations in a temporary world, is the first step to truly finding your confidence in middle school.

The best part of growing up is becoming comfortable in your own skin, being at home in the body God gave you, and being proud of the young woman you are. This Scripture even says that we are to be "at home" in our bodies, but there is something even better.

True confidence comes from walking by faith, not by sight. If we walk in what we know is true, and not what we "think" or "feel," nothing—not even death—can steal our confidence. One day, these earthly tents of ours are going to give out, and in that moment, who we truly are will be set free. All that will be left is the palace that God has built within us. In that moment, we will be in His presence, face to face, and we will know as we are known. In that moment, there will be nothing left to hide. In that moment, all that will matter is what is inside us.

In that moment, I want to be confident that who I am inside is nothing to be ashamed of. I would so much rather have a beautiful soul than a pretty face. I would so much rather have a gift for compassion than for art, music, or athletics. I would so much rather be obsessed with my Savior than anything this temporary world has to offer.

A life like spent in the pursuit of God will be unforgettable. If you are letting your Savior build a palace within the walls of your soul, nothing else will matter.

You will laugh at the future.

You will withstand any storm.

You will walk into this dark world armed with strength.

You will not slip on your path to the future.

You will run on the high places.

You will be the palace where God lives.

And, sister, no one will ever take that away from you.

CHAPTER 10

Outside In
Daily Study Guide

DAY 1

Read Psalm 45:13

A. Who is the King's daughter? How does this verse describe her?

B. Describe who you are on the inside in one word. Just one. I don't know about you, but I wouldn't describe myself with the word, "glorious." But that is exactly what Jesus intends to make us. We are His and filled with His glory and His Spirit.

C. What does it look like when someone is "glorious within"? Make a list of people you know who are "glorious within." Who are they? Why are they glorious within? And how can you follow God the way they do?

DAY 2

Read 2 Corinthians 5:4

A. What word describes our bodies in this verse? What is going to happen to this temporary life?

B. Our outer persona, or our "tent" is not always an easy thing to live with. What do you find to be the most difficult thing about your "earthly tent"?

C. Draw your heart dream house. What kind of palace do you want God to build within the walls of your heart? What beautiful character traits do you want Him to include?

DAY 3

Read 2 Corinthians 5:6-8

A. What two places are described in these verses? Fill in the blank: When we know we're heading for Heaven, we are "always _____."

B. What are three areas of your life where you are lacking confidence?

C. Get out your paper and make a plan. How are you going to walk by faith in those three areas this week?

DAY 4

Read Psalm 18:31-33

A. What four things does God do for us in this passage? Which one do you think sounds to the coolest?

B. What do you think it means to walk on the "high places"? Has God ever armed you with strength in a difficult situation?

C. Has the Lord ever taken you out of a difficult situation and set you on a high place? Be prepared to share this story with your group.

DAY 5
Read Psalm 18:34-36

A. What five things does God do for us in this passage? What has made us great?

B. Has the Lord ever been your shield, held you up, or kept you from slipping?

C. This is what confidence is meant to look like in our lives. Here's the beautiful part about these verses, it's not self-confidence, it's confidence in the Lord. Pray over the areas of your life where you are lacking confidence. Instead of praying for self-confidence, pray for the Lord to change you from the inside out, and help you to put your confidence in Him.

CHAPTER 11

What Dreams are Made of

Commit your way to the Lord,
Trust also in Him
And He will bring it to pass.

PSALM 37:5

A Chapter on Pursuing Your Passion

Dreams (Family Recipe)

INGREDIENTS

¾ c. Madness

2-3   Ideas That Will Never Work

2 c. Optimism

1ga. Creativity

⅔ c. Belief in the Impossible

1   Notebook

3ga. Perseverance

4 c. Passion

12   Ideas That Might Work

3.5k Sticky Notes (various colors)

      Pens (to taste)

      Blood, Sweat, and Tears (as needed)

DIRECTIONS

1. Using pens, combine madness, ideas that will never work, optimism, creativity, and belief in the impossible in a large notebook and set aside.

2. Cover ideas and allow them to rise for 2-3 weeks, or until a decent measure of reality sets in. Dreams should rise, doubling in size. However, not all dreams survive this process. If dreams do not rise, begin again from scratch, fixing where needed.

3. Fold perseverance and passion into dough until fully incorporated. (If perseverance is not mixed thoroughly, passion will evaporate while baking.)

4. Sprinkle ideas that might work evenly over sticky notes.

5. Place dough in the oven of reality for 3-5 years, or until fully formed. Administer blood, sweat, and tears as needed.

6. Test, fail, and retry periodically.

7. Enjoy!

Not Your Granny's Recipe

What are dreams made of? How do you take an idea and make it a reality? Which dreams come true? Which ones will turn out to be rubbish? And how do you tell the difference?

I had a lot of dreams in middle school. I wanted to write books for a living. I wanted to work with kids. I wanted to travel the world.

Every single one of those dreams has come true for me.

But there were other dreams too, dreams that never saw the light of day. Dreams that I had to let go of.

Today you and I are going to bake a batch of dreams. Get your apron, and prepare to get messy. Because dreams have a way of turning your world upside down.

We were created to be above-average teens in a world of complacency and apathy. Our dreams set us apart in our generation. Think of a particular dream. I know you have lots, but pick just one for right now. Make it a good one, a dream for the future that resides deep in your heart. Maybe no one else even knows it's there. What dream do you want to come true? Is it an artistic dream, an academic dream, a dream that helps other people? They all count! There is only one dream that doesn't count:

Rich and famous.

Now there is nothing wrong with wanting to be successful within your dream. Do you want to be an actor or a musician? Great. Do you want to create a business and see it do well? That's a wonderful dream, but our end goal should never be "rich and famous."

"Rich and famous" is not a dream. It's a Kardashian-fueled fantasy that has sidetracked too many teens and pre-teens of our generation. A life of luxury, ease, and popularity is a shallow goal, and you—beloved girl—were meant for more than that. The dreams of this world are temporary. You and I are were meant to dream dreams that last. This world wants us to settle for "rich and famous," but we were never supposed to fit into this world.

And do not be conformed to this world
But be transformed by the renewing of your mind

That you may prove what is that good
And acceptable and perfect will of God
Romans 12:2

Your dream is the secret whisper of your soul.

Your dream will be unique to you, different from everybody else's dream.

Your dream is what you were given to change the world.

The first thing any dream needs is room to expand and grow. That takes optimism, madness, creativity, and a few out-of-this-world ideas. Even if you don't have a specific dream at your center, you can find one. Start out by making a list of crazy dreams. These can be anything from adventurous foods to try (like octopus) to places to travel (like space). Write down a few of these ideas every day. Do you realize that if you wrote down ten ideas every day, you'd have seventy ideas every week, and three-thousand-six-hundred-and-fifty ideas every year?! If that doesn't get your creative juices flowing, I don't know what will.

In our teen years, it's important to dream big and not hold back. Be crazy. Let your imagination loose and see what you can come up with.

Prove it

You may have heard of dough that rises, but have you ever heard of dough that proves? In Britain, they call the "rising process" the "proving process." I love this term so much better because it defines the process more clearly. In the proving process, you set your dough somewhere warm to grow. If it works, then you're good to go. This process proves if you followed the recipe. It proves if you have all the right ingredients. It proves that the dough is everything it should be.

Our dreams need to go through a proving process. Once we've realized what it is we want out of life, we have to step back and see if the dream is going to last. This is an extremely scary and hard step, because not all dreams make it through this process. We might realize that our dream needs to be put on hold. Or we might decide that it's not what we want after all. The key to this proving process is all in where we put our dream. If we hold onto it, it's not going to rise. It needs a special place where it can grow.

What would you do if God showed up in your backyard?

That happened to a man named Gideon in Judges 6. God arrived to tell Gideon that He had a special purpose for his life. What did Gideon do? He made food. This is why I love Gideon. God shows up, drops an entire destiny on Gideon, and he's like, "Are You hungry? I'm hungry." Gideon worked for hours, making a perfect meal for the Lord. When it was finished, he set it before God. Guess what God did. He set it on fire. (I love the book of Judges.)

You see, Gideon thought that he was making a meal for the Lord, but when it came right down to it, his efforts became an act of worship, and his dream of making a meal for the Lord became a sacrifice.

Sometimes that's what our dreams are meant to be. Sometimes we'll spend years in an effort, and yet, when we set it before the Lord, it all seems to go up in smoke.

I've seen people go completely off track when that happens, thinking that they must have done something wrong. Gideon wasn't wrong for making a beautiful meal for the Lord. The Lord just had different plans for Gideon's dream.

When we develop a dream, we need to be willing to set it before the Lord, knowing that it could go up in smoke if it's not His will. If it's not His will for you, trust me, you don't want it. He is our God. He knows what is best for us. No matter how fond we are of our dream, we need to be willing to let it go.

Through the Fire

"How bad do you want it?"

This question gets thrown around a lot when it comes to dreams. The ambition fanatics would say that if you want your dreams to come true you have to want them more than anyone else wants them. That's not true. "Wanting it" will not make your dreams a reality.

I really want a glass of iced tea right now. I want it bad. I probably want it more than anyone else in my house right now. Wanting it is not going to make it happen. If I want that glass of iced tea, I need to get up off my backside. I need to go to the store. I need to buy iced tea. I need to be willing to put in the work. (Okay. Now I can't stop thinking about iced tea. I'll be right back.)

Slurps iced tea Despite what Hollywood wants you to believe, dreams don't usually happen overnight. They come one puzzle piece at a time. They morph and change and shift. They grow over the years, and they are worth the work. So many people are discouraged when they're not chosen, discovered, exonerated, or praised for their dreams. Don't fall into that trap. Stick with your dreams, and let the Lord change them over time as He sees fit.

Dreams are created in the secret places of our hearts, but they are forged in the fire. The dreams that survive the doubts and the fears and the hatred are the ones that change the world.

My brethren, count it all joy
When you fall into various trials,
Knowing that the testing of your faith produces patience.
But let patience have its perfect work,
That you may be perfect and complete, lacking nothing.
James 1:2-4

Even people who attain their dreams often feel that there is still something missing. That "special something" everyone else is missing is the hope that you and I have already found. Our dreams will be put through the pressure cooker of this life, and you and I need the strength and the perseverance to get through those trials and let God complete a perfect work of patience in our hearts. Once we let Him work His patience into us, we will lack nothing. We will be able to chase whatever dream He places in our path. We'll chase the next one and the next and the next one. When we learn to chase God's dreams instead of our own, we will find ourselves fulfilled and satisfied with His goodness.

Dreams come true.

Not when you wish upon a star.

Not when you want it badly enough.

Dreams come true, when you give your dreams back to your Creator.

Commit your way to Him, trust in Him, and He will bring it to pass.

CHAPTER 11

What Dreams are Made of
Daily Study Guide

DAY 1

Read Romans 12:2

    A. What are we not supposed to do? What are we supposed to do instead? Why?

    B. What does it look like when a girl is conformed to this world? What does it look like when a girl is transformed?

    C. How do our dreams set us apart in this world? How could the Lord use them to transform us?

DAY 2

Read Psalm 37:4

    A. What is the promise of this verse? What are we told to do?

    B. What does it mean to delight yourself in the Lord?

What can you do practically every day to delight yourself in Him?

C. Start creating your crazy idea list. Come up with things that you want to do in your lifetime. They can be fun things, crazy things, or just new things that you haven't tried.

DAY 3

Read Psalm 37:5

A. What is the process described in this verse? How are these three things connected?

B. Have you ever seen this process in someone's life? What does it look like when someone has committed their way to the Lord?

C. Get the list you created yesterday and put it before the Lord. Pray over it, asking Him to take away anything that is not His best for you. What on your list is hardest to give to Him?

DAY 4

Read Psalm 37:6-7

A. What six commands are listed in this verse? Which one do you find hardest to obey?

B. How can resting and waiting be part of our dreams? Why do you think that God commands us to do both?

C. What is a way that you could actively rest in the Lord as you wait for your dreams?

DAY 5

Read James 1:2-3

A. What are we to do when trials come our way? What does the testing of our faith produce? What does God want us to be?

B. Have you ever walked through a difficult trial? What effect did it have on your faith?

C. A true dream is one that you have the patience and the perseverance to see through to the end. Pray over the dream you've discovered this week. Pray over everything that could discourage you. Give your dream continually to the Lord, and ask for His will in your life.

CHAPTER 12

This Little Light of Mine

Let your light so shine before men,
That they may see your good works
And glorify your Father in Heaven.

MATTHEW 5:16

A Chapter on Keeping Your Sparkle

Fireworks

There is nothing in this world as fun as a sparkler. If your childhood was not complete with memories of fiery stick clutched in your sweaty palm raining sparks, happiness, and potential ER visits, you have my pity.

Talk about an adrenaline rush for a six-year-old. For an oldest child who was barely allowed to handle butter knives, Fourth of July was the one day a year that my parents willingly handed me a stick, set it on fire, and told me to enjoy.

I watched the sparks, showering the driveway. My favorite game to play with sparklers was "Letters." (My brother's was, "How Many Heart Attacks Can I Give Mom and Dad Before They Take My Sparkler Away?" A classic.)

As for me, I loved the magic of swirling my sparkler to spell my name in the air. I formed the swooping letters in the air, then I closed my eyes, and for a brief moment, my name would flash in the darkness.

Those smoky, warm summer evenings still make me smile. They were the epitome of my childhood.

All over the world, people are entranced by the magic of fireworks. Any good holiday needs them.

You'd think that after the hundreds of years that fireworks have been around, we'd get tired of them. Whether we're talking little sparklers or massive rockets that light the sky, when it comes to fireworks, we're all like little kids again, on the edge of our seats, waiting to see what will happen next.

That is the kind of breathless, childlike faith you and I were created to have.

> *You are the light of the world,*
> *A city that is set on a hill*
> *Cannot be hidden.*
> Matthew 5:14

You and I know that we are meant to be lights. We're not meant to be pale lamps, barely leaking out enough light for people to see our faith.

You and I are the sparklers of this world, and like my driveway on Fourth of July, our faith is not meant to be hidden. It's meant to be a shimmering, dancing display of joy for the world to see. Each firework is a little different from the others. They range in a rainbow of colors. Some crackle and boom, others sing. Each one is masterfully designed to give off a particular show.

You and I are no different.

Steal My Soul

In Chapter 2 we talked about your soul—your sookay. This is the part of you that lasts forever, the eternal spark that sets you apart from the rest of creation.

This world will try to steal your soul from you. Oh, not just your eternal soul. If you gave your life to Jesus, your soul is safe in the palm of His hand. However, as you grow up, this world will try to steal that sparkle. As your dreams and desires shape you into the young woman God create you to be, this world will try to dull your passion and make you like everybody else. Being like everybody else can get you a lot in this world. You'll be more popular. You'll have more money. You might even win the world over. The price for a life like that, is your soul, your sparkle, that part of you that makes you unique.

> *For what does it profit a man*
> *If he gains the whole world and loses his own soul?*
> *Or what would a man give in exchange for his soul?*
> Matthew 16:26

The best part of middle school is finding your sparkle, that part of you that is different from the rest of the world, that side of you that shines in the darkness of the world.

What is your sparkle?

Is it your imagination? Your creativity? Your organization? Your leadership skills?

Don't worry. Sometimes, we can't see our own sparkle, but we can see other people's.

In Acts Chapter 2, the Holy Spirit descended upon the

disciples. For the first time, they could feel God's presence living inside of them. When that happened, a rushing wind filled the room, and fire appeared over each of them. No disciple could see the flame above their own head. They could only see the Holy Spirit shining in the lives of those around them. That is how the work of the Holy Spirit is. If we could see our own sparkle, we would become self-centered. That's why God gave us each other.

Do you see God at work in the lives of the girls around you? Tell them! As sisters in the Lord, it is our job to tell one another how we see God at work in the lives of those around us. Sometimes, in this dark world, our sparkle gets a little weak. That is why God gave us each other. Stand alongside the young women God has placed in your life, and encourage them. Give them that extra little push they need to continue on their race of faith. Now and then, we all need someone to remind us how we sparkle like lights in this dark world.

For the Glory

What does the word glory mean? We hear it in church a lot. We also hear it when we talk about the fact that people want power, money, and glory. It's more than just pride, or credit. Glory means honor or renown, but it also means magnificence, beauty, and worship. We often hear about God having glory, but Romans 8 tells us something interesting.

For I consider that the sufferings
Of this present time are not worthy

To be compared with the glory
Which shall be revealed in us.
Romans 8:18

In us.

Not around us. Not above us. There is glory to be revealed in us.

According to this verse, you and I have glory hidden inside of us. There are several places in the Scriptures that talk about this glory. It's also called "dynamos" (pronounced doo-na-mus). Does that word look familiar? That's because we use it in English too. It's where we get our words "dynamic" and "dynamite."

In other words, when we get saved, the power of God is placed inside us like a stick of dynamite, waiting to be ignited. When we follow the Holy Spirit and let God work through us, we get to see little sparks flare and shimmer. When we pray over someone and see God at work in their lives, we get to see a little, Heavenly fireworks show.

For a child of God, every day is Independence Day. We have been set free from the powers of death and darkness. God has set us in Heavenly places and given us His Holy Spirit as a promise of our future with Him. And *that*, sister, is reason to party. We are walking around, carrying the very fireworks of Heaven. The sad part is, we can live our whole lives without setting off a single flare. That's not the kind of life I want to live.

I want to shine like a light in the universe.

I want to dance and shimmer in the goodness of God's grace.

I want my joy to be infectious.

I want to be a living firework.

Church was never meant to be a chore. Bible study was never meant to be one more class.

Our faith was meant to be the greatest party of all time, an invitation to everyone on earth. Our God brought hope, and—just like we learned in Chapter 1—He has empowered us to do the same.

Go Sparkle

Do not waste another day, beloved girl. In your hot, sweaty, little hand you hold enough hope to set the world on fire. Don't be afraid. Wherever you are, whatever neighborhood of the world the Lord has placed you in, you plant those feet in your driveway, and you shine. You sparkle and dance in a way that will make your God smile. You use every gift, every talent, every moment God has given you, and you shine like the confident young woman I know you are. You are not alone, beautiful girl. All over this world, daughters just like you stand in their own driveways and swirl their own little lights. You take that burning pen in your hand, and you tell this world what Jesus has done for you. Don't be ashamed of the beautiful young woman He has called you to be. As you and I form our sparkler stories, the Name of Jesus will flash in the darkness and light up this broken world.

Stand in the confidence that God has given you, and set the sky on fire with your joy.

Don't hide it.

Don't let this world steal.

Don't let Satan blow it out.

Let it shine, let it shine, let it shine.

CHAPTER 12

This Little Light of Mine
Daily Study Guide

DAY 1

Read Philippians 2:4-5

A. What are we commanded to do? What does the Lord want the world to call us? What does verse 5 compare us to?

B. Have you ever gotten to share the Lord with a friend who noticed that you stood out from the crowd?

C. Our faith was meant to shine and sparkle. What are ways that you, as an individual or you as a group, could actively be an example of joy to the unbelievers in your life? Come up with a list of ways that you can celebrate the freedom we have found in Christ.

DAY 2

Read Matthew 5:14

    A. What are we? What can never be hidden?

    B. Have you ever seen a city at night from a distance? Why do you think Jesus used that as an example of what we should be?

    C. Spend time with your Bible study group or a group of friends this week, and tell them how you see God at work in their lives. We can't always see what God is doing in us. We need our sisters' encouragement.

DAY 3

Read Matthew 5:15

    A. What should you never do with a lamp? Where does it go? Why?

    B. Have you ever met someone who hid the Light of Jesus instead of sharing it with others?

    C. It's not always easy to be a light-bearer. Sometimes we get tired and discouraged. This week, send a note of encouragement to one person in your home, reminding them of how much Jesus loves them. Give light to all who are in your house this week.

DAY 4

Read Matthew 5:16

    A. Why should we let our light shine? What is this world supposed to see when they look at us? Who is supposed to get the credit?

    B. Share about a time when you let your light shine.

    C. It's hard, and sometimes scary, to let your light shine. Are there times or places where you are afraid to share your faith? Spend time in prayer, asking God for boldness in these areas.

Day 5
Read Romans 8:18

A. What two things aren't even worth comparing? We discussed what glory is in the last chapter. Can you remember the definition?

B. Wow. I cannot believe that our time together is almost over. I have had so much fun with you as we've searched for our confidence together. It's been a wonderful twelve weeks! I cannot wait to see the glory that shall be revealed in you, sweet daughter of His. Don't be ashamed of who you are. Shine for Him. Shine boldly.

C. What have you learned about confidence in the last twelve weeks?

IF YOU DON'T KNOW JESUS

Just Us Girls is designed to build you in your faith and encourage you as you walk with God, but I know that some of you who are reading it do not know Jesus Christ as your personal Savior. I know this because I have prayed for you, prayed that God would put this book in your hands so that you can find out Who He is.

This Bible study is full of advice, tips, and ideas that help us to live Godly lives, but you know what? They are all pointless if Jesus Christ is not the Lord of your life. Without Him it doesn't matter, because without Him we can't find our true identity, we can't possess true joy, and we can't truly live out our destiny. It doesn't matter how good we are. We've all fallen short of God's glory (Romans 3:23). We all need forgiveness.

I don't know where you're coming from. Maybe you've never set foot in church. Maybe church is your life. Maybe you are desperate to find faith. Maybe you're a church kid who's wondering if you really believe this thing. Whoever you are I want you to know that Jesus Christ loves you with an everlasting love.

No matter who you are.

No matter what you've done.

No matter who has hurt you in the past.

No matter how many times you've heard it.

He loves you. He took special care as He created you. He's watched you as you've struggled and stumbled. He holds your every tear in the palm of His hand. He thought of you with His dying breath.

He doesn't want us to handle life on our own. We can't do this without Him, and He knows that. Faith is all about letting go and putting our hope in a God Who has promised to catch us.

Nothing else in life will ever fulfill us; not money, not fame, not romance. He is everything we long for.

If you would like to give your life to Jesus Christ today, just tell Him. Not sure what to say? This is something called the sinner's prayer. These aren't magic words. They simply cover the basics.

Dear Jesus,

I know that I'm a sinner. I've made mistakes. I know that I don't deserve to go to Heaven, and that nothing I could ever do could make me worthy. I believe that you are God. I believe that You died to pay for my sins, and I believe that You came back from the dead. Thank You for loving me. Do whatever You want with my life. It's Yours now.

In Jesus Name, Amen.

I so wish I could be there with you. I wish I could pray with you, but I want to hear your story. I want to know if you prayed that prayer. We are sisters in Christ now, and I am so excited to welcome you into this family! Please send me an email at authorhannahduggan@gmail.com. Let me rejoice with you. I love you dearly!

ACKNOWLEDGMENTS

Special thanks to the moms, Bible study leaders, and middle school girls who told me *Just Us Girls* needed a sister. This book would not exist without your reviews, emails, and encouragement. Thank you for your sweet comments and for encouraging this author to keep writing more books.

To my family for your constant encouragement and for making our home a place where dreams and books are born.

To Darien Gee who first spoke the fateful words, "What if you wrote a Bible study?" This book owes its existence to your coaching and support.

To my Savior, Who teaches me daily what it means to be His girl. I will follow You, and You alone, wherever You lead.

Let Your work appear to your servants
And Your glory to their children
And let the beauty of our God be upon us.
And establish the work of our hands for us,
Yes, establish the work of our hands.
Psalm 90:16-17

SCRIPTURE REFERENCES

Chapter 1:
2 Peter 1:2-3
Ephesians 1:6
Ephesians 1:4
Ephesians 1:19-20
John 10:10
Revelations 22:5
Isaiah 54:17
Proverbs 24:16
John 8:36
Psalm 102:12
John 15:11
1 Peter 5:8
2 Corinthians 2:11
Philippians 4:4
Philippians 4:7
Romans 8:28
Ephesians 3:12

Chapter 2:
Matthew 16:15
Matthew 16:25-26

Chapter 3:
Isiah 61:3
Exodus 20:17

Chapter 4:
1 Peter 3:4-5
Romans 8:28
Hebrews 13:5
Isaiah 61:3
1 Peter 1:4-5

Chapter 5:
Ephesians 3:18-19
1 John 4:18

Song of Solomon 2:10-12

Chapter 6:
Proverbs 12:26
Proverbs 27:6
Philippians 2:14
Proverbs 16:28
Proverbs 29:11

Chapter 7:
Psalm 31:3
Matthew 18:15-16

Chapter 8:
Matthew 7:7-8
James 1:5-6

Chapter 9:
Proverbs 29:11
Jeremiah 17:9
1 Corinthians 10:4, 5

Chapter 10:
Psalm 45:13
2 Corinthians 5:4
2 Corinthians 5:6-8

Chapter 11:
Psalm 37:5
Romans 12:2
James 1:2-4

Chapter 12:
Matthew 5:16
Matthew 5:14
Matthew 16:26
Romans 8:18

Hannah Duggan is the author of several works, including the bestselling devotional, *Just Us Girls*. As a Bible teacher, missionary, and youth leader, she spends her time investing in the lives of teens and young adults. When she's not writing or teaching retreats, she is serving at her church, Calvary Chapel Hamakua and spending time with her parents and two younger brothers.

To learn more about Hannah, her books, or her ministry visit www.authorhannahduggan.wordpress.com.

To get blog and book updates, free devotionals, and fun downloads, subscribe to her newsletter.

To get in touch with her or find out how she can connect with your Bible study group, write her at authorhannahduggan@gmail.com .

Just Us Girls:
A Bible Study on Being God's Girl in Middle School

Middle school isn't easy.

It's when you're figuring out who you are, who you hang out with, and what you believe. It's when friends become enemies and boys become...cute. It's obvious we need some girl time. I'll bring the discussion. You bring the chocolate.

We all need a day now and then when it's *Just Us Girls.*

Life gets tough. People get mean. How do we push through? What does God's plan mean for our lives? What does it mean to be God's girl in middle school? Well, that's what Just Us Girls is all about. Together we're going to search the Word of God and find out:

- who you were meant to be
- what to do about drama
- where to find a good friend
- how beautiful you really are
- why God picked you to change the world

DARE GREATLY
A High School Girl's Bible Study on Thriving in Your Teens

School. Eat. Sleep. Repeat.

Sound familiar? In high school, our lives fall into the same nerve-wracking pattern, but what if it didn't have to be that way?
What if stress and fear didn't dictate our decisions? What if we dared to do great things for God, not someday, but right now?
Because we were never meant to be "okay" girls living "okay" lives.

You are God's warrior. His secret weapon. His game-changer. This Bible study is more than a survival book for high school. *Dare Greatly* is a guide to discovering our God-given potential in our crazy, stressed out, homework-driven life. Because in Him, we have the ability to:

- Live Our Lives Exceptionally
- Conquer Our Fears Courageously
- Run This Race of Faith Dauntlessly
- And Dare Great Things for the Kingdom of God

WHAT NOW?
A Young Adult's Practical, Spiritual, And Somewhat Unusual Guide To Finding God's Will

As young adults, we question every decision. We live in the fear that our futures will crash and burn. We're terrified of messing up and missing out. Our lives are characterized by hard questions, and we're disillusioned with cliché answers. But what if I told you that you're right where God wants you? What if I told you that He's not afraid of your hard questions? What if I told you that God's will is right front of you?

What Now? is equipped with practical tools, spiritual breakthroughs, and somewhat unusual tips on how to find direction—not just for our futures—but in every area of our lives. If we dared to live the life God offers us, we could:

- Abandon our insecurities
- Break free of the lies that deny us our destiny
- Forge relationships that last
- Take on the future fearlessly

The greatest revivals in history started with a few young adults who took God at His Word. There is no end to what He can do when we're brave enough to ask Him, *"What Now?"*

Made in the USA
Las Vegas, NV
31 December 2021

39872816R00114